BIKE SCOT- LAND BOOK ONE

D0583004

The author and publisher have made every effort to ensure that the information in this publication is accurate, and accept no responsibility whatsoever for any loss, injury or inconvenience experienced by any person or persons whilst using this book.

published by
pocket mountains ltd
Holm Street, Moffat, DG10 9EB
pocketmountains.com

ISBN: 978-0-9544217-8-6

Text copyright © Fergal MacErlean 2005
Photography copyright © Pocket Mountains Ltd
Format and design © Pocket Mountains Ltd

The right of Fergal MacErlean to be identified as the Author of this work has been asserted by him in accordance with the Copyright, Designs and Patents Act 1988

A catalogue record for this book is available from the British Library

All route maps are based on 1945 Popular Edition Ordnance Survey material and revised from field surveys by Pocket Mountains Ltd, 2004-05. © Pocket Mountains Ltd 2005.

All rights reserved. No part of this publication may be reproduced, stored in a retrieval system, or transmitted in any form or by any means, electronic or mechanical, including photocopying and recording, unless expressly permitted by Pocket Mountains Ltd.

Printed in Poland

Introduction

The independence a bike gives you is immeasurable, whether you're into day-long trips or two-hour jaunts. Much of the fun derived from cycling is in seeing new parts of the world. That's where Bike Scotland comes in. For Book One, the author has biked the length and breadth of central Scotland seeking out the choicest, cycle-friendly routes that allow the rider to travel unhindered through some of Scotland's most diverse terrain, from the wave-swept beaches of the Atlantic west coast to the glens and straths of the north and east.

This guide contains forty routes of varying difficulty and length, ranging from an easy 10km to a committing 140km. All of the routes pass through fantastic countryside and each starts within an hour's train ride or so from the cities of central Scotland.

U2's Bono describes cycling as 'a Zen-like experience'. I think there's something in that: the whoosh of your tyres as the bike responds to your volition and the satisfaction of a long, well-earned downhill – Zen-like indeed.

Combine this with a train ride, as Bike Scotland does (all forty routes start and finish at train stations), and you've got the perfect, environmentally sound recipe for a day out, without the stresses of a car journey.

The majority of the rides are circular, starting and finishing at the same train station. Some use two stations to enjoy the best scenery, some involve ferries and a couple may require an overnight stop: hardly a hardship, though, considering the

locations. Many of the trips follow sections of the excellent National Cycle Network (NCN), a safe, smooth-surfaced and well-signed network of routes co-ordinated by the charity Sustrans. Only a few off-road excursions require a mountain bike, but in most cases the author has devised non-technical routes which can be followed on wide-tyred bikes.

All routes have been described to minimise uphills and maximise the descents, finishing with a downhill section where possible, preferably next to a pub. The overriding consideration has been to create journeys which follow a natural route through the landscape, with the minimum of turns, allowing for speedy and fun progress.

Using this guide

Of course this book is only intended as a guide. There's always the option of doing the best or more family-friendly bits of a route, as indicated in the text where appropriate.

The routes in this volume cover an extensive but accessible part of Scotland, from Arran in the west to Dunbar in the east and Loch Rannoch in the north. The opening section for each of the five regions introduces the area, topography and cycling highlights, alongside brief route outlines.

Each route has an introduction covering the level of difficulty, relevant Ordnance Survey (OS) map, total distance, average time and a brief note on access by train.

A contoured sketch map shows the route and key features of the area. This map is given as an aid to planning only: the relevant OS map should be taken on the trip. Detailed NCN maps are available from Sustrans (sustransshop.co.uk), who also offer an interactive mapping facility on their website (sustrans.org) and an information service on 0845 113 00 65. Other maps by Spokes: the Lothian Cycle Campaign (spokes.org.uk) and Glasgow Council's Fit for Life map are also invaluable.

Every route has an estimated round-trip time (based on an average flat road speed of 15kmph) which includes one or two very short stops and additional time built in for any ascent: this is for rough guidance only. Bear in mind that a strong wind will sap your energy and speed. Consider reversing route order on the day.

Also highlighted at the start of each route is terrain type and mountain-bike-only routes where applicable.

Access and cyclists' rights

You don't need to worry about access problems with any of the forty routes described. However, it's good to know that Scotland has a modern access framework, the best in the UK, for walkers, cyclists and other outdoor users, and one to which many other countries will aspire. The passing of the Land Reform (Scotland) Act 2003 enshrines the right of responsible access to the countryside with exclusions only to areas such as residential property, military installations and non-residential buildings and associated land. The Scottish Outdoor Access Code – a freely available government-published code of practice – details the do's and don'ts. As a rule of thumb, access for cyclists is allowed on byways, bridleways (restricted byways), unsurfaced, unclassified roads and forestry commission surfaced forestry tracks.

The CTC (the UK's national cyclists' organisation) and other national cycling bodies have contributed to the achievement of such a healthy state of affairs for cyclists

A word of advice for on-road cycling, by day or by night. You have as much right to use a road as the frustrated driver behind you. Don't be forced into the gutter where a pothole or drain may cause you to crash. Your safety comes first but remember at all times: a driver who can't see you won't slow down.

Taking the train

ScotRail, which operates most of Scotland's trains, encourages cyclists and bikes can be carried on all of their services for free. Because space is limited, it's a good idea to make a booking beforehand: between two and eight bikes can be carried on the long-distance services. Reservations can be made at principal staffed stations or by calling 08457 55 00 33. If you're travelling with children let the station staff know if you need assistance. ScotRail (scotrail.com) also offer a free cycle rescue service: see website for details.

East Coast and Virgin also operate some trains in Scotland, including (as far as it relates to this guide) Edinburgh to Dundee via Kirkcaldy. Tandems are generally not carried on trains in Scotland.

The cycle routes described start from the most convenient platform: this may mean having to carry your bike up and over sets of stairs or using the lift. Assistance may be available; otherwise additional route finding will be required.

Each trip is accompanied by an introduction, noting the major stations in central Scotland which offer direct access to the start or finish of the route. This is not an exhaustive list and it is worth checking information before you leave home. Of course, it is possible to drive to the start of these routes or at an appropriate point further on, but if doing so please park sensitively.

What you need

Any bike will do, except on the few routes where a mountain bike is specifically recommended. On-road routes incorporate quiet off-road cycle paths where possible. Unless indicated, these sections are suitable for all bikes, although a tourer provides a good compromise between speed and versatility.

As for clothing, most will do the job: it's up to you how comfy you want to be. Padded shorts may help to cushion your behind and padded gloves are always useful. In summer, shades are a good idea to keep out the flies; in winter a scarf or high collar and gloves are a must. All year round, take waterproofs and overshoes.

Make sure you have lights on your bike, even in summer: it's better to be safe than sorry. For routes that follow roads, use reflectors and reflective clothing too.

On shared-use paths, tracks and towpaths, be considerate and warn others of your approach with a bell or a friendly shout, especially when children or dogs are about. It makes good sense if cyclists keep to the left as a rule. Take particular care when passing under canal bridges and make sure anglers know you're about.

Do make sure if you have a child on the back that they wear a helmet and their seat is secure and suitable for their weight. And remember, on colder days they'll soon freeze as they're immobile.

Wear tight-fitting trousers or bicycle-clips and your chain will leave you in peace. Regularly check your brakes and watch out for frayed cables at tension points. Carry a spare tube, pump, puncture repair kit and wheel-nut spanners, if required, as a minimum. Without them, getting a puncture, even on a short spin, can be a drag.

On the more remote routes, carry a multi-tool with chain link remover, spare cable and cable ties too. Let someone know where you're going. Carrying a mobile is wise but not foolproof.

Fuel. Never leave home without it. Even on a short-spin you'll be glad of a few calories and a drink. If you're taking kids, it's a must.

That's it. Ready for a beautiful day?

The area around Glasgow is a playground for outdoor lovers. In no time, you can leave the city behind to find unexpectedly wild and rugged cycling country, world-famous lochs and islands and mesmerising views to boot. Within the city itself, there are several possibilities for peaceful traffic-free cycling. Glasgow City Council produces an excellent map (Fit for Life). The best city routes follow the canal and spur to Speirs Wharf, the Kelvin Walkway, the Clyde Cycleway and Sustrans' routes in the south side.

There are plenty of options on Glasgow's doorstep too: in this chapter, one ride follows a car-free circuit along country tracks, riverside paths and the Forth & Clyde canal from Milngavie (frequent train services from the city centre) on the northern fringes of the city.

Taking the train on the West Highland Line is an experience in itself. It runs from Glasgow's Queen Street station, to follow a route by the Clyde estuary and through the Loch Lomond & The Trossachs National Park, passing the Arrochar Alps before sweeping round by the northern end of Loch Lomond in just over an hour. Several of the routes use this line for a return leg.

A shorter train ride to Balloch at the southern end of the loch gives access to a range of routes, varying from hard off-road mountain biking to a Sunday spin in Scotland's first national park. The new Loch Lomond Cycleway along the west shore gives safe cycling through ancient oak woods, while the quiet roads of the eastern shore combined with a ferry crossing make for an exciting and memorable trip.

If you fancy the salt air in your face take a train to Greenock, Largs or Ardrossan. All routes from these points carry minimal traffic. Hop on a ferry and you'll soon be enjoying the distinct charm of island life and perfect cycling country. The island of Great Cumbrae is great for a fun and family-friendly cycle tour, while Arran provides the setting for an extended calf-pumping circuit around the northern half of the island.

Glasgow, Loch Lomond and the Clyde Islands

Arran and the Incredible String Road

Time 6h + ferry 2h **Distance** 68km
Terrain Hilly; minor roads **Map** OS
Landranger 69 **Access** Direct train from
Glasgow Central to Ardrossan Harbour;
ferry to Brodick

**This is a testing trip because of its hilly
nature. It follows the north coast road but
is generally very quiet, even in season.**

Arran is a gem, with its rugged mountain
ridges and relaxed air: few islanders are in
a rush. The island is ringed by a coastal
road, some 90km in circumference. For
much of this journey, the route follows the
northern part, skirting around the
mountainous interior before cutting across
the island on the challenging String Road,
so called by sailors for its offshore
appearance. Depending on your preference,
you can go for a one-day trip (58km/5h) or
spend a night overnight en route and take
time to visit the standing stones of Machrie
Moor (68km/6h). If travelling by car to

Arran in peak season, book your outward
and return ferry journeys in advance.

Start from Ardrossan Harbour: the train
terminates near the pier for the ferry to
Brodick which takes an hour. Disembark,
and turn right, remembering to stock up on
provisions here, particularly on Sundays or
out of season when few eateries are open
along the way. Follow the road inland to the
junction with the eastern end of the String
Road. The route soon returns to the shore
where it continues past the stately Brodick
Castle and Gardens and under Goatfell,
which is composed of a red coarse-grained
granite weathered into bizarre pinnacles
and gullies. Goatfell stands at the
southeastern end of two back-to-back
horseshoe ridges which include the peaks
of Cir Mhór and Caisteal Abhail. Pass
through the pretty village of Corrie and over
the River Sannox. This is a good spot to
charge your batteries for the tough 5km
climb ahead on a rough surface. Halfway

◀ Approaching Arran

along, after you cross the river, the gradient increases. But you can look forward to coasting down Glen Chalmadale to Lochranza on the north of the island (a lovely place to stay, with ferries to the Kintyre Peninsula for an extended tour) (2h). The next 10km are flat where the road hugs the coast. To the left the ground rises steeply, out to the right lies Kintyre: the winds can be strong along this section. Continue to Machrie Bay (3h30). [Variant: for a shorter journey, turn onto the minor road that leads back towards Brodick.] Carry straight on, passing the golf links to reach Machrie Moor after 1km. A 20-minute walk will take you past small rounded stone circles to the imposing Bronze Age standing stones: the setting is magnificent at the heart of an open valley. Back on your bike, keep south to reach the village of Blackwaterfoot with its tiny harbour (4h), where you should refuel before attempting the String Road (B880). This starts easily enough before swinging east and climbing to 230m in a little over 5km. The views of Arran's mountains make up for the effort, though, as you get a totally different

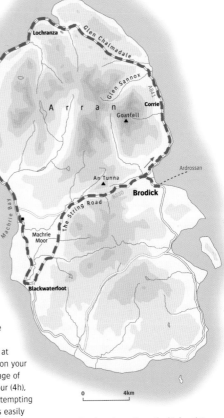

perspective from here. From the high point, the road drops into several tight bends before spitting you back onto the main road by Brodick Bay.

Bute and the Cowal Peninsula

Time 4h30 + ferries 1h Distance 75km
Terrain Hilly; quiet main roads; minor roads
Maps OS Landranger 55, 56 and 63
Access Direct trains from (outward)
Glasgow Central to Wemyss Bay and
(return) Gourock to Glasgow Central;
ferries from (outward) Wemyss Bay to
Rothesay, (onward) Rhubodach to
Colintraive and (return) Dunoon to Gourock

**Starting with a warm-up on the level
Isle of Bute, this route crosses into
mainland Argyll for some long but
satisfying road cycling with three ferry
crossings to add an adventurous frisson.**

Start from Wemyss Bay: the train
terminates by the Caledonian MacBrayne
ferry pier, where a 35-minute ferry ride will
take you into the heart of Rothesay on the
Isle of Bute. An option could be to spend
a night here exploring the surrounds at
your leisure. Otherwise follow the flat-as-a-
pancake coast road out of town. After Port
Bannatyne, turn right for Colintraive to
cycle by the Kyles of Bute ('Kyle' meaning
'narrow' or 'strait', from the Gaelic Caol).
At the end of the road at Rhubodach,
a five-minute ferry crossing to the mainland
takes you into Colintraive. The landscape
becomes hillier from here, but with the sea

air in your face for a while longer it's not a hardship. Take the first left to follow a short parallel section of the old road. Continue to Clachan of Glendaruel, which is marked by a lonely looking hotel (1h30). Follow the old minor road by the hotel to cross over the River Ruel and head up the glen. Eventually this brings you back out on the main road. Keep going uphill for about 5km through Caol Ghleann ('narrow glen') before swinging around for the descent to Loch Fyne. At the junction with another main road, turn right for Strachur, where there is a café and shop: this is the most northerly point of the route (3h). From here it goes south on the A815 for Dunoon. Thankfully, it's an easy enough 18km after the earlier hard work. A long on-road stretch follows the east shore of pretty Loch Eck which has two good inns on its banks (the more northerly has a bunkhouse). The rougher off-road Loch Eck Shore Trail can also be followed from Glenbranter to Benmore. Turn right by Ardbeg for views of Holy Loch, an inlet of the Firth of

Clyde and submarine base. As you approach Dunoon, take the harbour road all the way to the ferry terminal at the southern end of town. From there, it's a 25-minute crossing to Gourock and the train station.

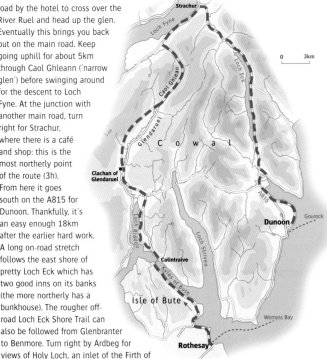

◄ Rothesay at dusk

An easy day on Cumbrae

Time **1h30** + ferry **20 min** Distance **16km**
Terrain **Flat; minor roads**
Map **OS Landranger 63** Access **Direct train
from Glasgow Central to Largs; ferry from
Largs to Great Cumbrae**

**The perfect outing for families with
young children on the accessible island
of Great Cumbrae.**

Glasgow's favourite summer day retreat,
Great Cumbrae is great at any time of year
for a short, quiet cycle: the kids will be
relieved that it's so flat too. Lying a 10-
minute ferry ride from the seaside town of
Largs on the Ayrshire coast, it couldn't be
easier to get to. On arrival, its island charm
is instant. The name 'Cumbrae' is possibly

derived from Gaelic, meaning 'shelter'.
While the island is indeed sheltered from
the brunt of the Atlantic winds, at the end
of the Firth of Clyde, and with the Isle of
Bute acting as a buffer to the west, families
would be advised to choose a calm day to
enjoy this route, particularly if travelling
with young children.

From the train station in Largs, head
north to reach the main road, or bear west
to the esplanade, both of which lead
northwards to the ferry pier for Great
Cumbrae. On arriving on the island, turn
right from the ferry slip to Tomont End,
where King Haakon of Norway based his
army camp on the eve of the 1263 Battle
of Largs. Go past this point to round Great

◀ Disembarking at Great Cumbrae

Cumbrae's northern tip in minutes. The shore road faithfully follows the island's 16km circumference and is as flat as any hill-hating cyclist could hope for. Rocky ridges dropping down from the interior add visual interest as do the beech groves and pockets of hazel and willow nearer to the road. The island's rocky west coast is the wildest and most scenic: it provides plenty of good picnic spots for enjoying the views and the wildlife. There is little habitation along here, apart from an outdoor centre, offering various activities, and tearoom. Great Cumbrae is home to shelduck, eider duck and barnacle geese and, if you're lucky, you might spot the odd seal too. Before you reach the town of Millport, you're treated to some of the best views on the island: Little Cumbrae stands offshore to the south and, beyond, the jagged mountains of Arran scratch skyward. Human life is concentrated in Millport, a Victorian seaside resort which hosts a Country & Western festival every year. A short distance back from the seafront is the Cathedral of the Isles, said to be the smallest cathedral in Europe – it seats 100 souls – though the attached collegiate

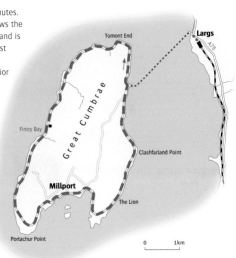

buildings make it look much bigger. Completed in 1851, it was commissioned by George Boyle, the 6th Earl of Glasgow, who was keen on rejuvenating the Episcopalian movement in Scotland. A later minister was said to be fond of offering up a regular prayer for 'the Great and Little Cumbrae and the adjacent islands of Great Britain and Ireland'. The town is stretched around the beautiful Millport Bay, which the road follows before heading north again. Look out for a geological dyke, aptly named The Lion Rock, on the way back to the ferry slipway at the start.

Above Greenock and the Clyde

Time **2h** Distance **14km** Terrain Hilly;
mostly minor roads; best for wide-tyred
bikes Map OS Landranger 63
Access Direct train from Glasgow Central
to Greenock Central

**Just a short train ride from Glasgow, the
moorland behind the Clydeside town of
Greenock offers challenging climbs
on a straightforward route with a
spectacularly scenic and swift descent.**

From the modest height of 200m above
sea level, there are extensive views of range
after range of hills which blend magically in
the Atlantic light. On a good day, you'll see
peaks on the Cowal Peninsula, the Mull of
Kintyre and, beyond, the Paps of Jura.

From Greenock Central station, follow the
stairs from either platform to Terrace Road
and go uphill. At the top, turn left down
Regent Street to a busy junction: it's easiest

to dismount and cross the road to continue
uphill to the right. Next, turn left onto
Ingleston Street following the Kilmacolm
Road (B788) signs. The climb begins in
earnest once you turn onto Kilmacolm
Road. It's a pretty steady ascent all the way.
Soon the town is left behind and you gain
a bird's eye view of the Clyde below. After
a lookout point, the road swings inland past
Harelaw Reservoir and Devol Moor.

A substation on your left (4km) marks the
end of any climbing. Looking south now,
you can see the extensive moorland of
Clyde Muirshiel Regional Park, which
stretches south from Greenock to Largs and
beyond. Drop southwards along a windy
stretch of road, passing a turn-off to
Kilmacolm. Slow down to take the next
right into the park, signposted for Loch
Thom. After passing stands of oak, you'll
enter pine forest where the road rapidly

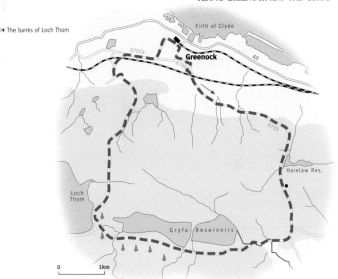

◀ The banks of Loch Thom

deteriorates into a rough, potholed track as it takes you past the Gryfe Reservoirs. At a junction, sweep right to reach the surfaced Old Largs Road. Turn right onto this to run by the eastern edge of Loch Thom, keeping your eyes peeled for hen harriers and peregrine falcons; short-eared owls, although predominantly nocturnal, may also occasionally be spotted during the day. [Detour: turn left onto this road and then right for refreshments at the Cornalees Centre, one of several visitor centres in the Regional Park, on the opposite side of Loch Thom.] This quiet road is a joy to follow as it climbs uphill for a short stretch before levelling out to give the first tantalising glimpse of the tips of the Argyll hills. The road swings briefly to the northeast where Ben Lomond and the Campsies come into view. Turn a final corner for the full breathtaking vista out to the islands off the west coast. Now comes 3km of swift descent to test the best of brakes and put the wind in your hair. When you reach the end of Old Largs Road at a T-junction, go right, still downhill. Continue round a sweeping right-hand bend and to a cross-roads, where you should turn right, signed Drumfrochar Road. After a pub on the left, take the third left onto Lynedoch Street and follow it down to a T-junction. Turn right into Regent Street and take the second left onto Terrace Road. Dismount to walk the short one-way section back to the station.

Rough Guide to the Campsies

Time **4h30** Distance **43km**
Terrain **Flat; cycle paths; rough in parts**
Maps **OS Landranger 64**
Access **Direct trains from Glasgow Queen Street/ Central to Milngavie**

Following a variety of tracks, cycle paths and rough pathways, this circular route from Milngavie to Kirkintilloch is full of interest for the determined off-the-beaten-track cyclist.

Start from Milngavie train station and find the start of the West Highland Way (marked by an obelisk) in the town centre. This long distance trail to Fort William is for walkers, but cyclists are welcome to use appropriate sections. Where the West Highland Way splits from the path to climb steps, keep to the lower path which follows the Allander Water. After 400m follow the sign to the

right for Mugdock Country Park Visitor Centre. Go left at the next junction, rejoining the West Highland Way and continue to a minor road where you leave the way. Drop into your lowest gear and turn right. Two hairpins later will bring you onto level ground with views of Ben Lomond. Turn right into Khyber car park to continue across moorland with views over Glasgow. Pass the formidable Mugdock Castle and then Mugdock Loch, turning left at a junction. Then at a T-junction, go right to exit the park. Turn right onto a minor road and take the next left onto Old Mugdock Road for a 2km quiet road section to Strathblane. At a T-junction go right, then left, and right again by the Kirkhouse Inn. Find the Strathkelvin Railway Path by a car park: this flat path runs all the way to Kirkintilloch. In Kirkintilloch a series of

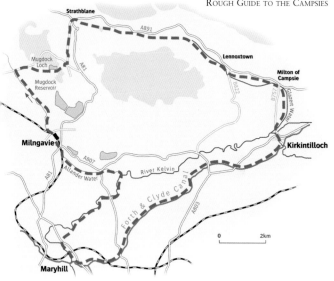

Strathblane

A891

Lennoxtown

Milton of
Campsie

Mugdock
Loch

A81

B822

B757

Mugdock
Reservoir

Glazert Water

Milngavie

Kirkintilloch

A807

River Kelvin

Allander Water

A803

Forth & Clyde Canal

0   2km

Maryhill

steps leads to a road. Cross this, go down a lane and over Hillhead Roundabout. Follow Canal Street to reach the Forth & Clyde towpath and head west by the canal for an easy 10km. Where the canal branches, follow signs for Bowling. About 1km further on, you reach Maryhill Locks. Ahead, leave the towpath for the Kelvin Walkway. Go ahead, heading for Milngavie, to pass under the Kelvin Aqueduct and continue until you reach Maryhill Road. Cross into Maryhill Park. At the crest of a hill, go right to enter a grassy section with views of the rolling Campsies. A path leads you round to an exit onto Caldercuilt Road. Turn left, passing a barrier where the road ends to leave the city behind and continue on a track. Go right at a fork to rejoin the Kelvin

where the journey upstream on narrow paths is now better suited to mountain bikes. This becomes more pleasant as you leave the worst of the undergrowth behind, and the path widens before a road crossing. On the far side of this, continue to the point 1km further on where the Kelvin loops east and the path now turns left to follow the Allander Water. A series of stiles and more undergrowth hinder your progress until you emerge on a minor road. Cross this and go down a flight of (often overgrown) steps. A couple of minutes further on, the path widens to give a clear run onto Glasgow Road. Turn left, then right by a railway bridge (onto a closed road) and right again into a park and back to Milngavie town centre.

◀ The Campsies from Strathblane

A bonnie ride from Balloch

Time **4h** Distance **27km** Terrain **Hilly;
minor roads** Maps **OS Landranger 56, 57,
63 and 64** Access **Direct train from
Glasgow Queen Street to Balloch**

**There are great views to discover on
this strenuous circuit of mainly quiet
roads and cycle paths from Balloch
to Gartocharn.**

Balloch train station terminus sits by the
mouth of the River Leven, the egress for
Loch Lomond. It's a popular tourist spot and
a great place for watching water traffic
come and go: the nearby shorelines
command famous views of the loch.

Leave the station and go right over the
River Leven to follow National Cycle
Network (NCN) Route 7 signs on the left
into Balloch Country Park and onto rougher

tracks. At a T-junction, ignore the cycle
signs and go left to follow a more
rewarding path by the loch shore. Stop at
a boathouse, where the southern end of
the loch's largest island Inchmurrin appears.
Head inland on a winding path up to
Balloch Castle. Keep in the same direction,
away from the loch, to pass through a
crossroads. You are now back on NCN Route
7. Follow the signs out of the park, across
the A811 and onto a minor road, which
rises steeply in a series of bends. The
gradient eventually eases, but many miles
of undulating ground still lie ahead. At a
sign for Gartocharn, leave the NCN and turn
left to head north: the perspective is now
more interesting as the dumpling-shaped
Duncryne hill and behind it, Conic Hill (both
remnants of volcanoes), come into view.

◀ On the banks of Loch Lomond

Further on, it's hard to mistake the solid shape of Ben Lomond by the eastern shore of the loch. The road drops steeply to the village of Gartocharn. At the junction with the busy main road, take a left turn, then first right. Soon the road swoops down towards the water. Go left by a grassy triangle and postbox, following signs for the Loch Lomond National Nature Reserve on a 1km-long rideable path. From various points, there are excellent views of Loch Lomond and its magical wooded islands. The surrounding marshland is an important sanctuary for snipe, curlew, redshank and goldeneye. Larger birds include migrant osprey and hundreds of over-wintering greylag and pink-footed geese. Back on the bike follow the road around the corner. After 1.5km turn right onto a smaller road which leads back into Gartocharn. Go left for about 50m and cross the main road to take the first right, which climbs steeply by Duncryne. Further on, take a right turn signed NCN Route 7 Caldarvan. Then, at a T-junction, go left, leaving the NCN again. Continue uphill to a crossroads and go right. A long 4km stretch follows, which will drop you down into Jamestown. Turn right to cycle along a busy road for 1km. Go through, or walk across, a roundabout and turn left at the following junction to return to Balloch train station.

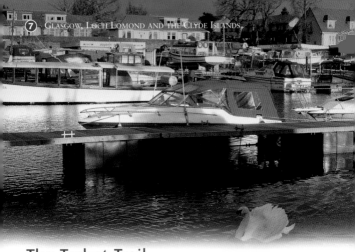

The Tarbet Trail

Time 2h30 Distance 28km Terrain Flat;
minor roads; cycle paths Maps OS
Landranger 63 and 56 Access Direct trains
from (outward) Glasgow Queen Street to
Balloch and (return) Arrochar & Tarbet to
Glasgow Queen Street or change at
Dumbarton Central for Balloch.
A new cycle-carrying bus service
(lochlomond4bs.co.uk) runs in the summer
months from Balloch to Tarbet, providing
an easy return from points en route

**This cycle path follows sections of an
old main road, from Balloch, at the
south end of Loch Lomond, to Tarbet, in
the heart of the Arrochar Alps, passing
through many of the wilder sections of
the loch's western shore.**

From Balloch train station, turn right and
then left through a car park and into a park.
Continue to the National Park Gateway
Centre. Pass Drumkinnon Tower and the
information centre on your right and carry
straight on to find a cycle path by the edge
of the car park. This leads to Old Luss
Road. Go right to soon follow the A82.
A considerable stretch of this route runs
by the busy main road. However, the route
is always separate from the road on a
dedicated cycle path. And it's more than
worthwhile for the quiet sections away
from the road, where you run alongside the
loch. At a roundabout for Cameron House
Hotel take the second road to run past
Duck Bay Marina for the first views of the
loch proper. The loch's largest island
Inchmurrin lies off shore; straight across
you can see the wooded southern edge of
the loch and behind rises Conic Hill, the
remnant of a once fiery volcano. The route
heads back up to the A82 and onto a path,
past the Arden roundabout and the Midross

◄ Boats at Balloch

development and golf course. After this, the route veers away from the road for a fun, windy section that runs parallel to another of Loch Lomond's many islands, the verdant Inchtavannach. At a T-junction, keep right for the old road. The countryside opens out as you approach the pretty village of Luss with its backdrop of rounded hills (1h). It's worth going to the end of the pier for the views both up and down the loch. On the

northbound road out of Luss, take the turning on the right to the Lodge Hotel and find the cycle path again as it drops down by the loch shore. The character of this body of water changes as it narrows and to the left the hillside steepens. When you come to the small pier at Inverbeg, bear round to the left and take an upper path. Ben Lomond looms across the loch and ahead juts Rubha Mor. This is the best bit as the route passes the deep waters of the loch, flanked here by ancient Dalradian schists. The last section, into Tarbet, is best done quickly as it's back by the road. Bear left onto the A83 for the train station, on the West Highland Line, just off the road on the right further ahead.

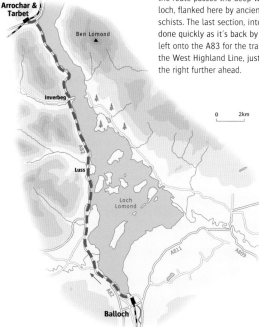

Over the hill to Cardross

Time 2h **Distance** 10km **Height gain** 200m
Terrain Hilly; rough track; minor roads;
suitable for mountain bikes only
Maps OS Landranger 63 and (optional) 56
Access Direct trains from (outward)
Glasgow Queen Street to Balloch and
(return) Cardross to Glasgow Queen Street
or change at Dalreoch for Balloch

**This short mountain bike route of two
halves offers a difficult climb above Loch
Lomond from Balloch with superb views
of the southern part of the loch, before
descending to Cardross.**

From Balloch train station turn right and
then left through a car park and into a park
which leads to the National Park Gateway
Centre, a curious mix of upmarket shops
and modern architecture. Pass Drumkinnon
Tower by the loch shore and information
centre on the right a bit further on. Go
straight ahead, along the edge of a car park
on a cycle path to reach Old Luss Road.
Turn left, pass a track to a ruined house and
take the next right, a narrow opening by
houses with a sometimes overgrown right
of way sign into Lower Stoneymollan Road.
Cross a footbridge over the main road and
continue uphill, a taste of what's to come,
with woodland on your left. Soon the road
turns into a jumbled stone track: it follows
the remains of an old wall and offers plenty
of testing moments. Throw in a couple of
burn crossings and you have quite a

challenge to stay on the bike, especially if the ground's wet. Persevere, though, and you'll be well rewarded when the path levels by the edge of pinewoods. This is a natural place to stop and appreciate the view and the Highland Boundary Fault, which traverses Scotland from Stonehaven to Arran and lies just about under your feet here. To the north lie some of the world's oldest rocks, which form the highlands; to the south lie younger sandstone and lava extrusions. The fault is best appreciated as a line running through the islands of Inchcailloch, Torrinch, Creinch and Inchmurrin and over the top of Conic Hill. Back in the saddle, the going is far easier

and you are nearly at the route's high point. Pass a large flat stone known as the Cross Stone. In times of old, this was used as a resting place for coffins carried by burial parties travelling between Luss and Cardross. Leave the woods behind after about 500m and join a small road which runs past Blackthird Farm. Take the next left and follow this round to the right for a blistering descent to Geilston. At the main road, go left and find Cardross train station in 500m on the right. There's a direct service to Glasgow but to return to Balloch by train, change at Dalreoch. Alternatively, retrace the route for a fun descent.

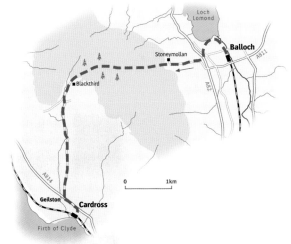

◀ On the road to Geilston

A Loch Lomond odyssey

Time 5h + ferry 15 min **Distance** 45km
Terrain Mainly flat; minor roads, cycle
paths **Maps** OS Landranger 63, 56, 64 and
57 **Access** Direct trains from (outward)
Glasgow Queen Street to Balloch and
(return) Tarbet to Glasgow Queen Street or
change at Dumbarton Central for Balloch;
summer ferry from Rowardennan to Inverbeg

**Explore the magic of Loch Lomond's
quieter eastern side. Spending a night in
Balmaha or at Rowardennan Youth
Hostel is recommended. The route is
described to Tarbet; a slightly longer
option is to return to Balloch.**

From Balloch train station, go right to
cross the River Leven and follow National
Cycle Network (NCN) Route 7 signs on the
left into Balloch Country Park and onto
rougher tracks. At a T-junction, ignore the
cycle signs and go left to follow a more
rewarding path by the loch shore. Stop at
a boathouse, where the southern end of the
loch's largest island Inchmurrin appears.
Head inland on a winding path up to
Balloch Castle. Keep in the same direction,
away from the loch, to pass through a
crossroads. You are now back on NCN Route
7. Follow the signs out of the park, across
the A811 and onto a minor road which rises
steeply in a series of bends. The gradient
eventually eases. The route is well signed
and carries on past Lochend Cottage and
Mavie Mill. After Pirniehall it runs

A LOCH LOMOND ODYSSEY

onto a dismantled railway, crosses through Croftamie and continues high above the Endrick Water. Join a road and go left, steeply uphill, then cross the A811 by a footbridge to reach Drymen, leaving the NCN route behind (2h30). Follow the B837 to Balmaha, which can be busy in season. From Balmaha a minor road runs to Rowardennan (4h). It's worth travelling outwith the peak season or at quieter times in the day to get the most out of this beautiful woodland stretch. An excellent diversion is to hire a boat or take the two-minute ferry ride from Balmaha Boat Yard to the island of Inchcailloch (Island of the old woman), minus the bike. Saint Kentigerna, an Irish missionary, is said to have lived here in the eighth century, hence the name. Up until 1670, mainlanders rowed across for mass and continued to bury their dead here until 1947. Like all of the main islands in the loch, it is heavily wooded, but paths cross the island, leading to a sandy beach. Continue on the winding road to reach Rowardennan Hotel and nearby youth hostel, where the public road ends. On route there are plenty of beaches and points worth stopping at. A diversion on foot to Ross Point is recommended. The

hotel runs a ferry service, three times daily, to Inverbeg on the loch's western shore from the end of March to the end of September. Book bikes beforehand if possible. On a quiet summer's day, the journey across the loch can be the highlight of the trip. From Inverbeg, this route joins the flat traffic-free Loch Lomond cycleway to run north to Arrochar & Tarbet train station, which is on the West Highland Line (about 9km). Alternatively, to return to Balloch and the low-level line, simply head south (20km).

◀ Loch Lomond from Rowardennan

Stirling lies at the heart of central Scotland, a varied area encompassing rich agricultural land and the rugged Trossachs. Stirling Castle is built on a volcanic outcrop and is a formidable reminder of the area's geographical importance, linking the highlands and lowlands of Scotland where the River Forth was once easily forded. Legendary battles fought in the area include the Battle of Stirling Bridge in 1297 when William Wallace repelled the English and, of course, the Battle of Bannockburn in 1314.

For the cyclist, the scenery around Stirling makes for a fantastic day out with the dramatic backdrop of mountains to the north and the nearer Touch and Gargunnock Hills to the west. The routes follow quiet country roads for the most part.

Many of the rides in this chapter start in nearby Dunblane (on the Glasgow to Perth line; direct trains also from Edinburgh) for easier forays into the Trossachs, where some of Scotland's best cycle paths are to be found. One route enjoys a traffic-free ride along the southern shore of Loch Venachar, another makes a circuit of the wonderfully peaceful Loch Katrine, both part of the Loch Lomond & The Trossachs National Park.

Longer routes include a venture on cycle tracks and minor roads to the eastern shores of Loch Lomond and beyond. A two-day epic, again on less used roads and cycle tracks, goes past Loch Lubnaig and Loch Tay into hidden glens.

To the east of Stirling, two routes from Falkirk make use of the Union Canal for a stress-free ride with surprisingly wild countryside in an area best known for its early foundries. A gleaming example of the area's pioneering tradition is passed en route: the engineering masterpiece that is the Falkirk Wheel.

Stirling, Falkirk and the Trossachs

Tour de Falkirk

Time **3h** Distance **31km** Terrain **Hilly;
towpath and minor roads**
Map **OS Landranger 65** Access **Direct
trains from Glasgow, Edinburgh and
Stirling to Falkirk High**

**Discover the delights of Falkirk's
countryside, from flowering bogs to an
awe-inspiring aqueduct, on this circuit
along reasonably quiet roads and tracks.**

Exit Falkirk High train station from either
platform. Platform 2 has access to the
Union Canal: follow signs and then look left
for access to Slamannan Road (by a fence).
From Platform 1, turn right on exiting and
first right to cycle uphill to the same road.
Turn left on to this and then right on to the
B8028 (Glenbrae). After a stiff climb, glide
downhill through a roundabout and into
Glen Village, then (just before a bend in the
main road) take a minor road on your right
to carry you across the Union Canal. About
1km beyond this, another short, steep climb

follows, ending at a T-junction where you
turn right. As you head west you get
increasingly interesting views of the
Central Uplands, but on rounding another
bend you find a changed landscape. Ahead,
as far as the eye can see, is flat bogland:
Gardrum Moss is on your left, while in early
summer Darnrig Moss (on your right) boasts
a white fluffy blanket of bog cotton. Beyond
this, at a T-junction, turn left to follow signs
for Avonbridge.

A long descent awaits. Cruise downhill to
join the B8022 and follow the signs along
undulating roads for Avonbridge. Once in
the village, turn left and then, after a pub,
turn right onto Blakston Road: this
is a peaceful winding road that follows the
River Avon for a pleasant 2km. The road
now swings away from the river, crossing
an old railway bridge: take care on loose
gravel. Further on at a T-junction, go right
on to a busier road and continue through
farmland to another junction, signposted for

◀ On the Forth & Clyde Canal

Candie. Take a left turn here and, at an unmarked T-junction after about 500m, turn right on to a quiet country road which leads to the A801. Cross over this to join a track just to the south, by a yellow barrier. This old estate track is quite rough and uphill at first (unsuitable for skinny racer tyres) but the path soon levels to meet the park entrance road after 500m. Turn right. For the visitor centre and a drink, carry straight on; otherwise take the first left towards a car park, then keep to the right to find a path which meets the River Avon. It's now a short ride downstream to reach the Avon Aqueduct – Scotland's longest and tallest – which carries the Union Canal. To get up there you must climb the Millennium Link,

80 steps up, to the end of the aqueduct. There's no need to cross the aqueduct except for the sheer hell of being high above the trees and the river (some 26 metres). [Variant: if you can't hack the steps, carry straight on (the path narrows) and bear right further on. Go right and take the first left after 300m onto Almond Road: this leads down to the canal where there's an access point on the right.] The route follows the canal (keep it on your left) for a pleasant 8km. As you near Falkirk, you will pass under a high arched bridge. Leave the towpath 100m beyond this, and follow an old ramp to return to the B8028 and the station. Alternatively, follow the canal through the sometimes unlit 631m Prospect Hill tunnel to return.

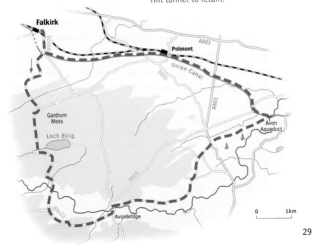

Around the Falkirk Wheel

Time **2h30** Distance **19km** Terrain **Mostly flat; towpaths and minor roads**
Map **OS Landranger 65** Access **Direct trains from Glasgow, Edinburgh and Stirling to Falkirk High**

Some surprisingly unspoilt countryside is to be found in Falkirk's hinterland, which this route passes through on minor farm roads and towpaths. Older traffic-confident children will enjoy this route and a trip around the Falkirk Wheel completes a great day.

Falkirk has been of strategic importance since Roman times. The Antonine Wall, spanning 59km from the Firth of Forth and the Firth of Clyde, passes north of the town. However, the Romans' most northerly defensive wall, initiated by the Roman emperor Antonius Pius in 138AD, failed to keep out the northern tribes. In 181AD they stormed the wall pushing the Romans south to Hadrian's Wall. Later, in the eighteenth and nineteenth centuries, Falkirk's iron foundries contributed to the beginnings of the Scottish industrial revolution. Falkirk was also, of course, at the centre of things when canals were at their commercial peak. The Forth & Clyde Canal was completed in 1790 and the Union Canal, a link canal from Edinburgh, joined it here in 1822. A recent revival in the fortunes of these canals has culminated in the revolutionary Falkirk Wheel, built in 2002. Boats are carried from the lower Forth & Clyde Canal to a height of more than 30m by way of an innovative rotating caisson. From there they join a spur of the Union Canal in mid-air. Boat trips on the world's first rotating boat lift offer the experience in full.

◀ High times on the Union Canal

Exit Falkirk High train station from either platform. Platform 2 has access to the Union Canal: follow signs and then look left for access to Slamannan Road (B803). From Platform 1, turn right on exiting and first right to cycle uphill to the same road, then turn right on to this and continue to a roundabout. Take the right exit onto Lochgreen Road to leave the houses behind. This minor road passes through farmland, making for easy cycling. Donkeys, marshland and some wild terrain give the route a distinctly west coast feel. Where the Ochils become visible, the road drops towards the Forth & Clyde Canal, with some steep sections for the last 2km. Go under a railway bridge and continue to the village of Allandale. Turn right and, after 500m, join the canal, part of the National Cycle Network, on your left. Cross at Underwood Lock to the towpath on the far side. The lockhouse is a fine place to stop for a drink or bite to eat on a good day. Continue along the peaceful canal to Bonnybridge. From there you can divert to the atmospheric Roman fort of Roughcastle. After a further 2km, the Falkirk Wheel comes into view. Cross the canal via a footbridge to the wheel and visitor centre (café). The footbridge is open during daylight hours; 24-hour access to the Union Canal is signed via Lock 16, by Camelon, to the east.

Although you have to pay to ride on the wheel itself, the sensation of travelling on water high above the ground is quite unique and the other facilities are free. Follow the path uphill past the wheel to enter a well-lit tunnel which passes beneath the Antonine Wall. One can imagine even the Romans would be impressed with the precision engineering of the wheel. Continue to follow the Union Canal all the way back to Falkirk. Falkirk High station is clearly signed and easily reached from the canal.

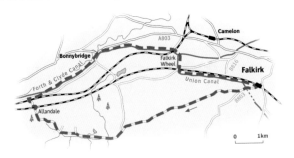

Stirling and the Carron Valley

Time 3h30 **Distance** 38km **Terrain** Hilly; quiet roads and town section
Map OS Landranger 57 **Access** Direct trains from Perth, Edinburgh and Glasgow Queen Street to Stirling

From the heart of Stirling, this circuit quickly escapes to the countryside for some tough but peaceful cycling through the Touch Hills — with some great downhills.

Start at Stirling train station, heading up the hill to turn left at a roundabout towards the city centre. When you reach a second mini roundabout, turn left to push your bike through a pedestrian section. Then go straight through the crossroads to reach Port Street. Take the first right to follow King's Park Road, passing an old-style cinema. Continue past King's Park and go straight ahead at a small roundabout onto Polmaise Road. After 500m, at a sign for Cambusbarron, turn right. The road crosses over the M9. On the far side, turn left: this marks the start of a long section of ascent, which passes through quiet countryside. After little over 1km, where the road sweeps west, the gradient eases. Continue, ignoring the turn-off for a small road to the left. Shortly beyond this, the road you are on plunges down to cross a burn: this flows into the Bannock Burn which rises nearby through the North Third Reservoir which you will soon pass. Another fairly long climb starts by a plantation. After a brief interlude on an easier stretch, the hill steepens again for a demanding haul past a scattering of houses. Eventually, you reach the top: most of the hard work is now behind you. Take the road to the left with its fine views over

e reservoir and the Sauchie Crags, one-
me home to an Iron Age fort. These lands
ere inhabited before that too: a Bronze
ge battleaxe was discovered when the
servoir was filled; it's now in the Royal
useum in Edinburgh. About 2km further
n, you'll come to a T-junction: the right
rn will bring you down to a B-road. The
nal section before the junction is
specially steep: be prepared! At a pub on
e crossroads, turn right and continue on
e flat, smooth-surfaced road that leads
u along the northern edge of the
npressive Carron Valley Reservoir. Where
e water ends, turn right onto a minor road

which weaves and steeply climbs its way up
onto the moor, now home to a windfarm.
You'll find a number of lovely picnic spots
beside the various burns that tumble down
the hillside. Soon after passing the Earl's
Hill communications mast, a rutted but
wonderful descent leads down to the
outward section of the route and you get to
enjoy descending the hills climbed earlier.
Some of these are very steep indeed and
will have you grinning on your way
back to Stirling.

Towards Loch Coulter Reservoir from Carron Bridge

Trossachs trail to Ardlui

Ardlui

Loch Katrine

Inveruglas

Loch Arklet

Loch Lomond

Inversnaid

Ben Lomond ▲

Loch Chon

0   3km

Time **4h** + ferry 10 min Distance **65km**
Terrain Mainly flat; A- and minor roads;
cycle paths Maps OS Landranger
57 and 56 Access Direct trains from
(outward) Edinburgh and Glasgow Queen
Street to Stirling and (return) Ardlui to
Glasgow Queen Street; ferry from
Inversnaid to Inveruglas

**This route from Stirling ends far from
the starting point, in Ardlui at the
northern tip of Loch Lomond, promising
a real adventure.**

It's remarkably flat too, crossing the
carselands to the west of Stirling through

which the River Forth meanders.
Much of this rich bogland was drained and
stripped for agricultural purposes, and it
is today the biggest hay-producing area in
the country. In places, this route carries
fast-moving traffic.

From Stirling train station go right and

ust after a zebra crossing turn right to cycle by the Tesco supermarket. Keep straight on through two underpasses, and by the Old Bridge follow the Raploch Riverwalk to join the A84. Turn right and go straight ahead through two big roundabouts:

long undulating section runs through Loch Ard pine forest and past Loch Chon. Where the plantation finishes, you abruptly enter a much wilder moorland landscape. The road runs by the end of desolate Loch Arklet to a junction. Go left for Inversnaid by the loch. The hair-raising descent to Inversnaid Hotel is memorable (there's a bunkhouse at

here is a path on the right hand side. ust after a garden centre, look for an old bridge on your left. Go over it to find a quiet road which winds through farmland. After km, go right at a T-junction onto the B8075 and then left. Turn left at the side road for Thornhill, and from there follow the Aberfoyle road west. This brings you north of Flanders Moss, an important wintering ground for thousands of pink-footed geese, and the Lake of Menteith, Scotland's only ake. After a few fun bends, you eventually reach another T-junction. Go right to shortly reach Aberfoyle (2h). You'll notice how the landscape has closed in and crags have appeared. Ahead lies some even more interesting scenery. Go straight ahead on the B829 to follow the infant Forth that lows through Loch Ard. Soon the road runs s close to the loch as possible, providing great views for the cyclist. Further on, a

the top) (3h30). Just as you come to a halt, you realise you've reached Loch Lomond. The hotel runs a ferry service to Inveruglas on the western shore of the loch: this is weather dependent with no fixed timetable, so make enquiries in advance. After disembarking, head north on Loch Lomond's busy A82 to the train station at Ardlui. There's a hotel there, but to really round off this trip it's worth staying at the charming Inverarnan Hotel 3km up the road. It's like something from Middle Earth! [Variant: There's also the option of reaching the Inverarnan on foot. Leave the bikes at Inversnaid and follow the spectacular walkers' only section of the signposted West Highland Way.]

All aboard at Inversnaid

Sheriffmuir and Ochil views

Time **2h30** Distance **14km**
Terrain Undulating; one long ascent; minor
roads Map OS Landranger 57 Access Direct
trains from (outward) Stirling, Perth,
Edinburgh and Glasgow Queen Street to
Dunblane and (return) Bridge of Allan to
Dunblane, Stirling, Perth, Edinburgh and
Glasgow Queen Street

**A surprisingly tough journey up into the
Ochils and down through fern-clad gorges
on quiet minor roads. This route starts
and finishes in the Victorian spa towns of
Dunblane and Bridge of Allan, which are
linked by a frequent rail service.**

Start at Dunblane train station. Cross the
Allan Water to head up High Street. Turn
right at the mini-roundabout, continuing
straight on at the next roundabout. Ahead
lies a long climb up to the wild moorland
Sheriffmuir. After 500m, the gradient eases
off as you leave residential Dunblane
behind. Turn left at the next junction. This
marks the start of another steep section,
rewarded, however, by views of Ben Vorlich
and Stuc a'Chroin on your left. Carry
straight on to pass waterworks and, soon
after, to begin a welcome downhill section.
This takes you past a memorial to those lo
in the Battle of Sheriffmuir, an indecisive

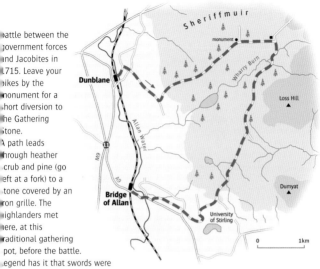

battle between the
government forces
and Jacobites in
1715. Leave your
bikes by the
monument for a
short diversion to
the Gathering
stone.
A path leads
through heather
scrub and pine (go
left at a fork) to a
stone covered by an
iron grille. The
highlanders met
here, at this
traditional gathering
spot, before the battle.
Legend has it that swords were
sharpened on the low-lying stone. Back on
the bike, continue uphill, now at a much
easier angle. The western edge of the
rounded Ochil Hills come fully into view.
Beneath them, at a junction, is the
Sheriffmuir Inn where overheated cyclists
will be glad to drink their fill or have a
meal. The inn, situated on an old drovers'
road, marks the high point of the route.
From here, go downhill to cross the
burgling Wharry Burn. A narrow winding
road guides you past fields of sheep and
stunted trees to pass Dumyat, a hill popular
with walkers, on the left, and a reservoir on
the right. A dip and subsequent rise follow
before a savage descent through trees. Slow

down where a road joins on the right
at a widening, and continue down a steep
gorge. At the bottom, on the level, pass
the walls of Stirling University, to come
to a T-junction. Turn right, uphill, onto
residential Kenilworth Road. Continue
straight on through the leafy Bridge of
Allan. After about 750m, the road joins
Well Road which leads downhill to the
main street. Turn right onto this to leave
the main part of this Victorian spa town.
After crossing the bridge over the Allan,
continue for 300m to find the pedestrian
entrance to the station. From here,
Dunblane is just minutes away by train,
which is preferable to the busy road option.

On Sheriffmuir

37

Loch Venachar by Callander

Time **4h30** Distance **60km** Terrain **Minor roads; quiet main roads; cycle paths** Map **OS Landranger 57** Access **Direct trains from Stirling, Perth, Edinburgh and Glasgow Queen Street to Dunblane**

This is a satisfying and straightforward level circuit, which explores the charms of the Trossachs in a day outing from Dunblane.

Located west of Callander, Loch Venachar lies by the Highland Boundary Fault. The fault extends in a diagonal line from Arran via Loch Lomond and the Menteith Hills to the south of Loch Venachar, continuing to Callander and all of the way to the east coast at Stonehaven. This route ventures into the Trossachs, north of the fault line, amidst a wonderful jumble of bumps and crags, interwoven with famous lochs.

Start from Dunblane for access by train,

ut nearby Callander also makes an ideal base.

Exit Dunblane train station on the west (Tesco) side. Turn right and follow the reasonably quiet A820 to Doune. In the centre of Doune, go left and left again at the next junction to cross the River Teith, then take a right and follow the upper road (B8032). At a junction after about 0km, go right along the A81. Just after houses, round a bend to take the minor Invertrossachs road on your left – part of NCN Route 7 – and follow the southern shore of Loch Venachar through oak woods. After just over 1km, the road narrows for a fun 3km stretch that sees little traffic, continuing past old waterworks at the loch's eastern end with views of the popular Ben Ledi to the north. As you enter the

Invertrossachs estate, the route veers right onto a car-free track which runs directly alongside the loch with plenty of excellent spots for a picnic. Further on, where the route joins a much larger forestry road, turn right to leave the NCN and continue for about 2km to a T-junction. Turn right towards a farmhouse, where you soon come to a cattle grid (you may need to cross a stile). An old stone bridge takes you over the Black Water to the charming Byre Inn. Turn right onto the A821, a gently undulating and fairly peaceful bogland road that leads you along the northern shore where you'll find the welcoming Harbour Café. Continue for about 1km, taking the next right over an old bridge. This rejoins the Invertrossachs road. Turn left to retrace your tracks to Dunblane.

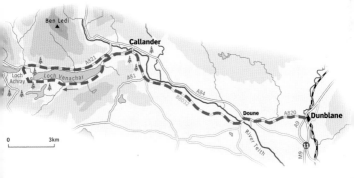

◀ Setting sail on Loch Venachar

Loch Katrine voyage

Time 7h Distance 85km Terrain Minor
roads; quiet main roads; cycle paths
Maps OS Landranger 56 and 57
Access Direct trains from Stirling, Perth,
Edinburgh and Glasgow Queen Street to
Dunblane; ferry from the Trossachs Pier to
Stronachlachar

**Cycling in Scotland doesn't get finer
than this route around the mesmerising
Loch Katrine. The steamer that forms
part of this circuit runs only in summer
and advance booking is recommended.**

Loch Katrine is set in magnificent
Trossachs scenery at the heart of Rob Roy
country (the famous red-haired outlaw was
born at Glengyle at the head of the loch).
There are few better introductions to these
waters than by the venerable SS Sir Walter
Scott, a century-old steamship which runs
a morning service from the Trossachs Pier
at the east end to Stronachlachar on the
far western shore. Check times and book
bike places before leaving home. Times
and distances given assume a start
from Dunblane and use of the ferry

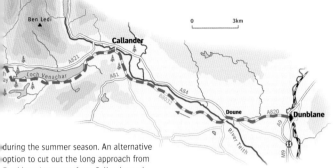

0   3km

Ben Ledi
Callander
A821
Loch Venachar
A81
A84
B8032
A821
Doune
A820
Dunblane
River Teith
A9
M9

during the summer season. An alternative option to cut out the long approach from Dunblane is to start from Callander and reduce cycling distance to 20km (2h). A variety of bikes can also be hired at the Trossachs Pier.

This route also makes a good two-day trip for those who want to take their time, stopping at the Invertrossachs Hostel by Loch Venachar en route. The less traffic-confident, however, should only consider the Loch Katrine or southern Loch Venachar sections.

To get there by train, leave Dunblane train station on the west (Tesco) side. Turn right and follow the reasonably quiet A820 to Doune. In the centre of Doune go left and left again at the next junction to cross the River Teith. Go right and follow the upper road (B8032). About 10km later, at a junction, go right along the A81. Just after houses, round a bend to take the minor Invertrossachs road on your left – part of NCN Route 7 – and follow the southern shore of Loch Venachar. [Detour: Continue straight on if you wish to stop for refreshments at Callander.] Further on, where the route joins a much larger

forestry road, turn right, leaving the NCN. Continue to a T-junction. Bear right and cross an old stone bridge by an inn. Turn left onto the A821 and head for the Trossachs Pier on Loch Katrine to catch the steamer (shop, tearoom and bike hire here). At Stronachlachar pier, disembark to follow the wonderfully traffic-free road clockwise round the loch. This 20km stretch should be manageable by the whole family so long as you have brought plenty of provisions: there are no shops after leaving the pier. The head of the loch is encircled by hills and it's easy to imagine Rob Roy delighting in this wild land. The first 8km or so are level; after this the road begins to undulate with some fairly steep sections, although you can walk these if necessary. If the steamer's not running you can always cycle from the Trossachs pier for as far as you fancy. To return to Dunblane you can follow the northern shore of Loch Venachar (café and chance to view ospreys on route) for speed, taking the first right after the loch back to the Invertrossachs road.

◀ SS Sir Walter Scott on Loch Katrine

Going wild in Glen Finglas

Time 8h Distance 80km Terrain Flat to
start, then hilly; Landrover tracks;
suitable for mountain bikes only
Map OS Landranger 57 Access Direct
trains from Stirling, Perth, Edinburgh
and Glasgow Queen Street to Dunblane

**This upland mountain bike route
explores the wilds of Glen Finglas,
reaching a height of 600m. It is a
challenging route which shouldn't be
attempted unless you are prepared for
changeable highland weather.**

Glen Finglas, which extends from Loch
Venachar to the top of Ben Ledi, is owned
by the Woodland Trust Scotland and is part
of the Loch Lomond & The Trossachs
National Park. The Trust is working to

The road to Glen Finglas

eforest the glen, once a popular hunting
ground of Stewart kings, with the aim of
establishing one of the largest native
broadleaved woodlands in Scotland. As this
is a strenuous day out, you might want to
consider an overnight stop if starting from
Dunblane. An alternative is to start from
Callander or from Brig o'Turk itself, cutting
the distance to 23km (4h).

To get to Brig o'Turk from Dunblane, exit
the train station on the west (Tesco) side.
Turn right and follow the reasonably quiet
A820 to Doune. In the centre of Doune, go
left and left again at the next junction to
cross the River Teith, then take a right to
follow the upper road (B8032). At a junction
go right along the A81. Just after houses
round a bend to take the minor
Invertrossachs road on your left. After 2km,
turn right to cross over a bridge and go left
alongside Loch Venachar to reach Brig
o'Turk. [Variant: for a slightly longer but
traffic-free route follow the southern shore
as described in the Dunblane-Loch
Venachar route (p38). Consider overnighting
at the Invertrossachs Hostel.] In Brig o'Turk,

at the western end of Loch Venachar, take
the road north. At a fork, after about 700m,
follow the upper road. A steep climb brings
you to a lookout point with the first
inspiring views across the Glen Finglas
reservoir. Soon after this point, the tarmac
road comes to an abrupt end, marking the
start of what is to be a pretty bumpy
journey. A wildly undulating landrover track
skirts around the edge of the reservoir.
Further on, ignore a track on the right: this
is the end of your return section which runs
on the far side of the high ground called
Meall Cala, or The Mell, as this route is
known. Derived from Gaelic, Glen Finglas is
thought to mean 'glen of the white water'
and you'll see how apt this is as you make
your ascent into the narrow upper reaches
by the surging Finglas Water. At a ford,
leave the burn to begin a serious climb
which will have you pushing your bike for a
considerable distance. Take heart that the
route does eventually traverse round to the
right at an easier angle. If you look carefully
you will see it in the distance, not that it
matters as you can't go wrong. A final push
takes you to the highest cairn-marked point.
Now comes the long descent that will leave
your fingers brake weary, before more
undulating ground by the Allt Gleann nam
Meann. No route finding is involved, apart
from one junction where you should follow
the road to the left. Shortly before dropping
back to Glen Finglas Reservoir, take time to
enjoy the fantastic views back over your
route. From Brig o'Turk, return to the start.

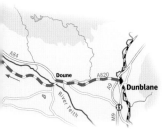

Grand tour of Loch Tay

Time 9h **Distance** 142km **Terrain** Flat
sections interspersed with very tough
climbs; minor roads; quiet main road; cycle
paths **Maps** OS Landranger 57, 51, 52 and
56; NCN Lochs & Glens Cycle Route North
Access Trains from (outward) Stirling,
Perth, Edinburgh and Glasgow Queen
Street to Dunblane and (return) Perth to
Dunblane, Stirling, Edinburgh and
Glasgow Queen Street

**This testing route heads north from
Dunblane on minor roads and good cycle
paths to Killin and Loch Tay. There
follows a stiff climb to secluded Glen
Quaich, and a final run into Perth down
Glen Almond.**

Exit Dunblane train station on the west
(Tesco) side. Turn right and follow the
reasonably quiet A820 to Doune. In the
village centre, go left and left again at the
next junction to cross the River Teith, then
take a right to follow the upper road
(B8032). At a junction, go right along the
A81. Follow this road over the River Teith
and, just before Callander's main street (1h),
go left onto NCN Route 7 which this route
follows to the eastern end of Loch Tay. This
is a fantastic ride, all on quiet roads or
cycle paths. To the top of Glen Ogle it
mainly follows the Callander-Oban railway
line. Initially, it winds through oak woods
before an easy stretch by the shores of Loch
Lubnaig. A climb takes you onto forestry
roads, which lead steeply down into a
tranquil glen and Balquhidder, at the heart
of Rob Roy country. Pass the beautiful Loch
Voil and go right at a T-junction. Further on,

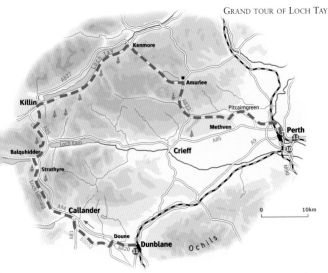

NCN signs point the way onto an old railway track on the left just before an underpass and the Kingshouse Hotel, which, incidentally, is a great place to get waylaid. The track runs parallel to the A84 before veering away to reach an ultra-steep hairpin section. After it, there's a steady incline up Glen Ogle crossing an old railway viaduct en route (allow three hours for Strathyre-Killin). At the top sits the lovely Lochan Lairig Cheile. Cross over, with the Tarmachan ridge ahead, through forestry and down into Killin. The route now takes a right turn onto a minor road, signed Ardeonaig, just before a pub. This road by Loch Tay's southern shore undulates in places but is ideal for cycling. Pass a recreated crannog (thatched loch dwelling on stilts) after Acharn (6h). A visit to the crannog centre is recommended. There's a

restaurant nearby too. Further on, don't join the main road at a T-junction but take a minor road on the right. This is a very steep stretch, from the word go, for 5km, though the gradient eases slightly after 800m. Pass Tombuie Cottage for another tough climb which eases gradually as you gain height. Pass a lochan and continue for another 2km to the high point in the wilds. Round a bend to find Glen Quaich laid out below you. Two very tight hairpins come next. Beware of ice: this road isn't gritted. Continue for 7km over undulating ground, past isolated Loch Freuchie. At a junction go left for the Amulree Hotel (7h30) or, to press on, go right on the quiet A822 for an easy stretch through Sma' Glen. Take the next left onto the B8063 to Buchanty. From here the route goes via Pitcairngreen to follow NCN Route 77 into Perth, as described on page 78.

◀ Downtown Killin

On the edge of the highlands, Pitlochry, Blair Atholl and Dunkeld are easily reached by train in about an hour from Stirling and just slightly longer from Edinburgh and Glasgow.

To follow the main Highland Line north up the centre of the country is to pass into a wide open landscape as the wooded hills and crags around Dunkeld, on the edge of the Highland Boundary Fault, give way near Blair Atholl to the dramatic open country just south of the Cairngorms.

It's great cycling country for the vistas and sense of freedom, and all routes have been chosen with traffic levels in mind. Where road travel is necessary minor roads are used, none of which are unpleasant, and most of these trips take advantage of the region's excellent cycle paths.

While all three start points are important tourist attractions, away from the honeypots of Pitlochry, Dunkeld, the Pass of Killiecrankie visitor centre and Blair Castle, you'll meet few people. In their place you'll find red deer, ospreys and red squirrels.

The routes in this section vary from full-day off-road mountain biking in the wild and remote Glen Tilt to a much more sedate, but eminently enjoyable, pedal in and around the Atholl Estate.

Two circuits take in the wildlife and woodland around Dunkeld. From Pitlochry, there is a wonderful circular tour of the much photographed Loch Tummel and a great outing to the Tay's most popular whitewater rapids.

Further down the glen, a circuit of Loch Rannoch, accessed from the West Highland Line, penetrates the fringes of the vast trackless moorland that is Rannoch Moor, passing ancient stands of Scots pine as it follows the lonely shoreline.

Highland Perthshire

The Loch of Lowes from Dunkeld

Time 2h Distance 22km Terrain Mainly
level; mostly minor roads
Map OS Landranger 52 Access Direct
trains from Perth, Stirling, Edinburgh and
Glasgow Queen Street to Dunkeld

**Following quiet minor roads and cycle
paths this is an easy circular route by
the Loch of Lowes wildlife reserve, a
haven for ospreys and other birds.**

Start from Dunkeld & Birnam train station
building, turning right onto NCN Route 77
southbound for 3km. This follows a
dedicated cycle path parallel to the A9,
which then joins a minor road where you go
right. After passing under a railway bridge,
take the next left, signposted for Murthly, to
leave the NCN and pass into gentle rolling
farmland and under the A9. This marks the
start of a quieter stretch, which continues
until very near the end of the route. Further
on, where the road steers you northwards,
you come to a junction and sharp bend:
bear left along a rough road to meet the
B9099 to Caputh. Turn left onto this where
it sweeps you downhill, over the Tay and
into the village. Now turn right at a
T-junction to follow signs for Coupar Angus

Downhill to Dunkeld

into the quiet A984. After passing a school, take the next left, signposted for Clunie. You're on minor roads again here, which are ideal for a summer's evening spin when there are no cars around. At a fork, 2.5km further on, turn left for Dunkeld, ignoring further turnings to arc gently westwards along quiet wooded roads. As you approach the Loch of Lowes, the hills of the Forest of Clunie comes into view. Skirt around the south side of the loch to reach the visitor centre. During the summer months, you can view ospreys at this breeding area, as well as many common woodland birds and wildfowl.

Ospreys, which have a wingspan of 1.5m, are the third largest birds of prey in Scotland after the Golden and Sea Eagles.

These migratory birds which visit during the summer months to breed were driven to near extinction in 1917. Now, after a 50-year reintroduction programme, they are again breeding successfully in Scotland.

Just beyond the loch and visitor centre, you join the main road at a T-junction. Turn left and keep to the main road for a swift descent through glorious pine to Dunkeld, home to the folk-favourite Taybank Hotel as well as a number of other good pubs and eateries. To return to the station, cross the Tay on Telford's arched bridge and turn left into Birnam, a pretty village which is almost a continuation of Dunkeld. Soon after, take a right turn up Birnam Lane, indicated by a blue NCN sign.

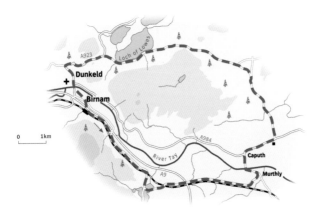

The Hermitage and dark Craigvinean

Time 2h Distance 18km Terrain Mountain
bike route; hilly; minor roads and tracks
Map OS Landranger 52 Access Direct trains
from Perth, Stirling, Edinburgh and
Glasgow Queen Street to Dunkeld

**A challenging ride on forestry tracks in
Craigvinean Forest by Dunkeld with a
varied start and level family-friendly
woodland finish. Around Dunkeld in
autumn swathes of the hillside turn gold
as Larch, a non-evergreen conifer,
prepares to lose its needles.**

Exit Dunkeld & Birnam train station,
turning left at the side to follow a stepped
path. Turn right and at the road go left. This
brings you to a T-junction where you follow
the underpass signs for Inver. Carry straight
on to reach a minor road and continue
uphill to Inver Car Park. Follow signs in the
car park to the Hermitage, a wooded area
on the banks of the River Braan. Take care
as this is primarily a walkers' path: it's
rough going at any rate. Cycle along the
river through pleasant woodland, passing a
Celtic carving, and cross an old stone bridge
near the Black Linn Fall. Ossian's Hall, a
folly built on a rocky outcrop on the far
side, frames the falls perfectly from within.
Head upstream for about 50m before
turning right onto a minor track, just before
a flagstone. This very shortly meets a large

upward-trending
path. Turn left
into this, passing
carved totem
pole, to reach
crossroads.
Another left turn
brings you to a
good forestry road.
This steepens as it
wends its way uphill
round Craig Vinean:
it is not for the faint-
hearted. After about
1km, take the first right,
where the views open
up over Strath Tay.
A brief fun section
follows where you glide
high above the A9, then it's
upwards again for 1km. Turn
right at a T-junction and, in just under
1km, beyond a small quarry, slow down to
look for a right turn: this marks the start of
a grin-inducing descent. Tight switchbacks
lead quickly down to a junction: ignore the
track on the right and turn left. More
corkscrews follow before you join a forestry
road, where you turn right. There are no
more directions to worry about and you'll
soon be on a smooth earth surface.
Descend, taking in a curve. The angle
steepens considerably as you turn a last
corner for 1km of pure descent. Keep an
eye out for walkers and other cyclists as
well as for the gate at the bottom. A right

turn now takes you onto a minor road, part
of NCN Route 77, which leads to the A9.
Ignore signs for Inver and go left to follow
the A9 over the Tay for 200m. The cycle
path then dips left to meet a level riverside
path, still part of the NCN, which is suitable
for all cyclists. On approaching the town,
signs lead past the Hilton Dunkeld. Follow
the hotel avenue to the main road and turn
right. This takes you back through town,
where there are restaurants, pubs and
shops to distract, or you can carry straight
on across the Tay, following signs for the
adjoining village of Birnam to return to
the train station.

◀ Autumn leaves in the Hermitage

Rapid ride to Grandtully

Time **4h** Distance **31km** Terrain **Hilly;
minor roads and brief A-road sections**
Map **OS Landranger 52** Access **Direct trains
from Perth, Stirling, Edinburgh and
Glasgow Queen Street to Pitlochry**

**This route takes you on an interesting
loop down to Grandtully and high above
the A9 on a hard climb for a swift
descent to Pitlochry.**

From Pitlochry train station, follow NCN
Route 7 south, signposted for Logierait.
This leads to Port na Craig, an ancient ferry
crossing for the monks of Coupar Angus,
which operated from the twelfth century.
It's now a suspension bridge that takes you
across the River Tummel, near the Pitlochry
Festival Theatre. Blue NCN signs direct you
under the A9, where you pass close to
Dunfallandy Stone, an ornate Pictish cross-
slab, on your right. The next undulating 4km
steepen considerably before descending to
Logierait. Here, a cycle path signed for
Strathtay takes you across the restored
Tay Viaduct and continues westwards.
This flat and very quiet section of the route
offers perfect family cycling. Further on,
cross a bridge to the north bank of the Tay,
continuing to follow Strathtay signs. At a
fork in the village, turn left to cross back
over the river to Grandtully, where you can
enjoy the spectacle of whitewater canoeing

◄ The former viaduct near Logierait

over a drink. Grandtully Rapid, one of the longest and most exciting rapids on the Tay, is an important canoe slalom site and also the end point for whitewater rafters hurtling downriver from Aberfeldy. Follow the road eastwards to return to Logierait. Here, you should leave the NCN to continue east, above the A9, to Ballinluig. After passing a garage, turn right at a sign for Dalcapon. This marks the start of a steep ascent. Just before a bank of trees, a minor road for Dalcapon leads left. Take this to continue to

climb for about 1.5km. There's a short level stretch before a hair-raising descent with some very tight bends. Take particular care on the first one where the road narrows, the gradient suddenly steepens and there's some loose gravel for good measure. After this there are other tight spots: keep in to the left. When you reach a T-junction, turn right for Pitlochry to reach an A-road; turn right again. It's now 2km into town, where you'll see signs for the station on the left.

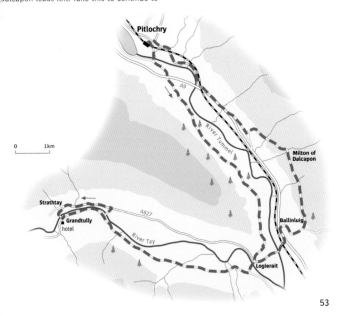

Tummel and freewheeling Faskally

Time **3h** Distance **41km** Terrain **Mostly
flat with some hills; minor roads**
Maps **OS Landranger 43 and 52**
Access **Direct trains from Perth, Stirling,
Edinburgh and Glasgow Queen Street
to Pitlochry**

**Following Loch Tummel's busier northern
road and returning on the minor
southern road, this great route passes
through some of the most majestic
scenery of highland Perthshire.**

From Pitlochry train station, follow the
main street northbound for Killiecrankie.

After about 4km, turn left to follow signs fo
Tummel Bridge and cross the River Garry.
Traffic can be quite heavy on this section at

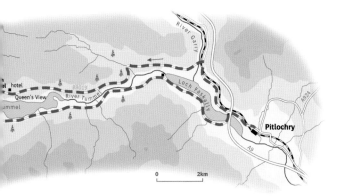

arious times, so it's worth doing this route
t quieter times if possible. Easy initial hills
may lure you into thinking this is going to
e a breeze, but some of the small rises
head call for some serious stamina.

ll that hard work is rewarded with great
escents through fine woodland, however,
omplete with exciting hairpin bends.

lext comes a longer ascent, the last of the
limbs for some distance, as you approach
Queen's View with aspects down the loch
o the iconic peak of Schiehallion. The
amed viewpoint is not named after Queen
ictoria, as many believe, although the
monarch did rest for tea near here in 1866
she got cold tea but enjoyed the views). It
s, in fact, named after Queen Isabel, the
rst wife of Robert the Bruce. Nowadays, a
offee shop gives everyone the chance to
njoy the views across the water. About
alfway along the loch, where there are far
ewer trees, you pass Strath Tummel with
ts roadside hotel. On this well-surfaced,
ndulating road, you'll find yourself at the

end of the loch in no time. Take the left
turning at Tummel Bridge and cross the
water, passing a power station as you climb
southwards, with Schiehallion to your right.
At the edge of a plantation, turn left onto
a road signposted for Foss, which is usually
free of traffic: this is a delightful section
which soon joins the southern shore of
Loch Tummel. Sail down to the water and
on through birch woods: there's plenty of
wildlife here, including buzzards.

When you're just about opposite Queen's
View, the route passes through more mature
trees as the road begins to rise past Clunie
Dam. Steep descents add some excitement
before you freewheel by Linn of Tummel,
Clunie Power Station and Loch Faskally.
Ahead of you, the A9 crosses by a
roadbridge. Instead of passing under this,
look to your left to find a footbridge which
takes you over to a track. Go right, past a
boating shed, and right again onto Clunie
Bridge Road. At the top, simply turn right
to return to Pitlochry.

Loch Faskally from the main road

Killiecrankie and the Soldier's Leap

Time **2h** Distance **15km** Terrain **Flat; one
long climb; minor roads and cycle path**
Map **OS Landranger 43** Access **Direct trains
from Perth, Stirling, Edinburgh and
Glasgow Queen Street to Blair Atholl**

**Running alongside the River Garry,
this route takes you through splendid
country before a testing climb and steep
descent to reach the legendary site of
the Soldier's Leap.**

From the northbound platform at Blair
Atholl train station, join a minor road via a
ramp: this soon turns into a track which

crosses the River Garry. Carry on downstream on the now well-surfaced track to
enjoy a blissfully flat section with views to
the hills behind Blair Atholl. Further on, the
track goes underneath the A9 where it joins
a minor road. Pass by farmland, still on the
level, with views of the small but plucky
Ben Vrackie. At a T-junction, turn right to
continue in a southerly direction, running
roughly parallel to the river, now some
distance away. The road climbs severely
from the start, the steep incline continuing
for about 1km.

It levels briefly as you near some crags,

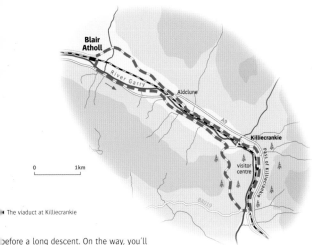

◀ The viaduct at Killiecrankie

before a long descent. On the way, you'll pass the old church and graveyard at Tenandry, the peaceful interior a million miles away from the rush of the A9. From here, the descent steepens to zip you through mixed woodland: this is red squirrel territory. Scotland is a haven for this popular native, supporting 75 per cent (121,000) of the estimated British total. But they are in danger, even here, of being pushed out by the introduced North American grey squirrel, which competes for food. The loss of natural habitat through extensive woodland felling has affected red squirrels while the more adaptable grey squirrel has exploited alternative food resources.

You shortly come to a rude stop at a T-junction. Turn left to cross the Garry Bridge with fabulous views of the gorge below. On the far side, turn left again to reach a minor

road – the Pass of Killiecrankie.

Further on, you can learn about the dramatic history of this once crucial pass at the visitor centre. An important Jacobite victory was won just north of this at the Battle of Killiecrankie in 1689. Of particular interest is the notorious spot nearby, known as The Soldier's Leap where a government soldier pursued by Jacobites is said to have outwitted his assailants by vaulting more than 5m across the Garry. Not to be tried on a bike! On the far side of the pass, you reach the little village of Killiecrankie. Continue straight through onto a long flat stretch that takes you back under the A9 before depositing you in Blair Atholl where the Atholl Arms Hotel is conveniently located next to the train station.

Glen Tilt expedition

Time **8h** Distance **53km** Terrain **Hilly;
landrover tracks; rough boggy paths;
mountain bike route (height gain 800m)**
Map **OS Landranger 43** Access **Direct trains
from Perth, Edinburgh, Stirling and
Glasgow Queen Street to Blair Atholl**

**This is a long and serious mountain bike
outing through the Atholl and Mar
Lodge estates, with a burn crossing that
may be dangerous in spate. Bring
provisions, map, compass, torch and
repair kit for a taste of Scotland's real
wilds. This route is best attempted in
drier weather when the going is easier
and erosion threats are reduced.**

From Blair Atholl train station, turn right
along the main village road and then left at
a minor road, signposted for Old Blair. Turn
left for Glen Tilt car park and find a track to

the north of this. The track leads above the
raging River Tilt, through woods and over a
bridge. Leave the trees behind for a 14km
long but easy upward-trending ride on
landrover tracks before the 'fun' starts. On
rough land, take care to minimise damage
by staying on the path and in ruts. Pass
Marble Lodge followed by a rise before
Forest Lodge where you pass through a
dense and dark stretch of pine. Now you
enter a wilder part of the glen. Look back
from a small wooden bridge over a side
burn to see the shapely Carn Torcaidh on
the northern side of the Beinn a' Ghlo
complex (1h30). About 1km further ahead,
at a fork, veer right. Soon the track
becomes a path: you'll need to walk part of
the 4km to Fealar Lodge; don't churn up
paths but walk over any waterlogged
sections. At the confluence of An Lochain

and the Tilt, you'll hear the melodious sound of gurgling water. Looking back down Glen Tilt in the right light, the river can give the impression of flowing uphill. Pass the Falls of Tarf on a Victorian suspension bridge. Ahead, leave the main path and swing to the right to continue across the burn (in spate, this can be dangerous) and follow the obvious steep earthen path up onto open moorland.

Variant: A time-consuming alternative is to cross the Tilt by a bridge 5km downstream (beneath Beinn A' Ghlo's Luib Mhór spur), following sheep tracks to rejoin the path to Fealar Lodge. If in doubt, contact Mar Lodge Estate (National Trust for Scotland) or Blair Atholl Estate.] Boggy sections hamper progress here. Continue to Fealar Lodge where there's a bothy (3h). A landrover track runs downhill for about 1.5km before a hard climb by Gleann Mór, compensated for by a 5km run down to buildings at Daldhu (4h30). After the second building, find a grassy track which runs northwest. Whatever tracks your map might show on this return section beneath Carn nan Gabhar and Carn Liath, the standard is poor and in places the path disappears.

Continue uphill for 45 minutes past Glen Loch on the right. The track peters out to a rough path 2km beyond the loch: take care to follow it. After you round Srón na h-Innearach, trending downhill, make sure you bear south (left), not southwest as this way, despite often being shown on maps, ends in failure. Cross a burn, and pass through a gate after 800m and onto a faint track to Shinagag. Go right at Shinagag, following a track to the northwest. Turn left back on the main drag: the hardships are now over. Cycle under Carn Liath and past some tin shacks to reach a better surfaced track. This leads onto a minor road, which swoops downhill for 4km to Blair Atholl with the promise of a roaring fire, beer and food in the Atholl Arms Hotel right by the station.

◄ Looking up Glen Tilt

The Falls of Bruar

Time **1h30** Distance **15km** Terrain **Level with one hill; tracks, B-road and minor roads; best for wide tyres**
Map **OS Landranger 43** Access **Direct trains from Perth, Stirling, Edinburgh and Glasgow Queen Street to Blair Atholl**

This is a mixed route on tracks, some steep, with great views and enjoyable cycling through the Atholl Estate.

Forest, rivers and hills clad in heather make up much of the 140,000 acres of the Atholl Estate. This route traverses some of the estate's lower forested slopes and takes in the wonderful Falls of Bruar. Mountain bikes are recommended as there are a couple of rugged stretches, but experienced cyclists can manage on wide-tyred bikes.

From the train station at Blair Atholl, go right and turn into Atholl Estate. Cycle up the avenue a short distance and take a right turn to come out by the Old Bridge of Tilt car park after 1.5km. Head west out of the car park, turning right at a fork and then left further on at a crossroads. Turn right at a

-junction onto a wide track, the West Drive, by a highland pony trekking centre. This gives delightful level cycling with views to match. A folly on the right adds to the grandeur of this historic home of the Earls and Dukes of Atholl. After about 2km, at a junction, turn right into mature pinewoods, now on a much steeper, rougher track. At a fork around 400m further, turn left to follow a smoother but still fairly uphill track, which eases off after about 1km. In autumn this section is littered with mushrooms and toadstools of all shapes and sizes. About 1km further on, where the road divides, turn left along the lower route for a sudden introduction to the magnificent Falls of Bruar. The larch and Scots pine which line the gorge owe their existence to Scottish bard Robbie Burns who entreated the Duke to plant the then bare slopes of the beautiful gorge in his poem 'The Humble Petition of Bruar Water'.

> Would then my noble master please
> To grant my highest wishes,
> He'll shade my banks wi' tow'ring trees,
> And bonnie spreading bushes.

The poet's request was carried out posthumously and though no trees survive from the original planting, the beauty of this 'wild garden' endures.

From the Falls, the track loops east to drop steeply downhill, passing under a railway bridge before reaching a road. Turn left on to the reasonably quiet B8079 (a right turn will take you to Perthshire's prestigious House of Bruar country store) and continue for just over 1km to reach the estate's West Lodge. Pass through the lodge gates, closing them behind you, to rejoin the West Drive. Return by the outward route to pass behind the striking white Blair Castle.

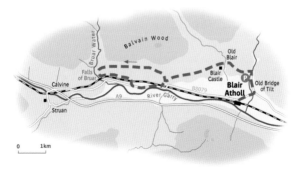

◄ Blair Castle

Loch Rannoch loop

Time **3h** Distance **51km** Terrain **Flat**
Map **OS Landranger 42** Access **Direct**
train from Glasgow Queen Street to
Rannoch Station

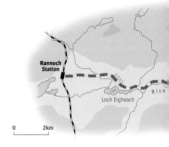

**Getting to this remote outpost is half
the fun on a spectacular train journey
followed by a level cycle around a fine
highland loch.**

The route starts from Rannoch Station on
the West Highland Line. One road runs to
the station from the east but in all other
directions lies the boggy wilderness of
Rannoch Moor. During the Ice Age, Rannoch
Moor's elevated position meant glaciers

formed there before sliding off into the
surrounding lands, forming the hollows
which later became water-filled as lochs.

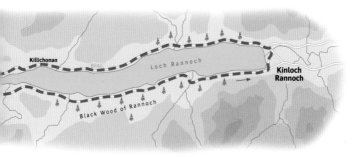

The ice also deposited rocks, known as erratics, far from their original location. In the village of Kinloch Rannoch, at the far end of this route, erratics have been used as a building stone. Look for speckled black and white blocks. They are granodiorite, a rock similar to granite, which came from Rannoch Moor.

Leave the station and follow the road across this beautifully stark landscape towards Loch Rannoch. On a good day, the peaks around Glencoe can be seen to the west while Ben Alder stands to the north. After about 8km, largely downhill, you'll come to a junction. Turn right and cross the River Gaur by a stone-built bridge to continue eastwards along the southern shore. This quiet road rises at first but then descends to the lochside with great views of the route ahead. After leaving the shore for a while, the road flattens entirely as it enters the lichen-drenched Black Wood of Rannoch, one of the largest survivors of the ancient Caledonian forest. Next stop is

Kinloch Rannoch, at the foot of the loch. The small village, which lies on the River Tummel with the iconic peak of Schiehallion towering behind, contains shops and hotels and is popular with walkers and cyclists. From here, it's an undulating journey through the hazel and birch woods that line the loch's northern shore on a slightly busier road. As you approach Killichonan near the head of the loch, the perspective opens up. Keep an eye out for the island and structure in the middle of the water: there was once a crannog (ancient loch dwelling) here; it is also said that locals used to hide out from their enemies on the island. Carry straight on at the junction to retrace your route to the station and catch that train. For those wishing to extend their stay in the area, a night or a meal at the Moor Of Rannoch Hotel, just before the station, could be an option. The station also has a tearoom (seasonal). Phone in advance to make sure they'll be open when you're there.

Remote Rannoch Station

Fife and lowland Perthshire have
plenty of wonderful, accessible countryside
for the cyclist. While lowland Perthshire
is resolutely agricultural, Fife is a mix of
disused coalmines, crop-growing fields,
pretty harbour villages and long golden
beaches. There are three distinct areas:
West Fife, the fertile Howe of Fife in the
middle, and the East Neuk which juts
into the sea.

Fifers are proud of their historical
importance – Dunfermline was Scotland's
ancient capital — and they stoutly defend
the popular county title 'the Kingdom of Fife'.

Modern-day Fife has what is probably the
most comprehensive cycle network in
Scotland, thanks to its extensive road
system. While some of the Kingdom's
cycleways carry fast-moving traffic, this
guide has sought out the least frequented
routes. The longest in Fife is the 150km-
plus Kingdom Route, a circular route
between the Forth and Tay bridges, which
also forms the Fife leg of National Cycle
Network Route 1 and the trans-European
North Sea Cycle Route. The rides in this
chapter include a journey along a disused
railway track and a peaceful coastal route
by a pine forest and less used minor roads.

The Perthshire outings are no less
enticing. From the buzzing town of Perth,
two trips explore the surroundings, from
lonely glens to breath-snatching descents.
Perthshire's claim to governance precedes
Dunfermline's: in 843AD, Kenneth
MacAlpin, King of the Irish Dalriada tribe
united the Picts and Celts and declared
himself ruler of Scotia at Scone.

West of Perth, starting close to
Gleneagles, a circuit makes an early
challenging climb and long final descent
through the eastern edge of the Ochil Hills.

Lowland Perthshire and Fife

Dunfermline to the Forth

Time **2h30** Distance **18km** Terrain **Mostly flat; cycle paths and minor roads**
Map **OS Landranger 65 or NCN Round the Forth Route** Access **Direct train from Edinburgh to Dunfermline Town**

A well-signposted ride from the historical town of Dunfermline via the pretty villages of Limekilns and Charlestown on the Forth.

Fife is one of Scotland's more farsighted councils as far as cycling goes, with a network of signposted routes across its low-lying terrain. Some, like this circular route, are far more cycle friendly than others, however. The circuit starts in Dunfermline and follows sections of both the NCN Route 76 and the Kingdom of Fife routes.

From Dunfermline Town train station, go through the underpass onto Comely Park. Go left to a junction and keep left to reach Priory Lane. Follow the road as it swings round to the left. On the right stands Andrew Carnegie's modest birthplace. It is now a museum to the 19th-century American steel tycoon turned philanthropist. Continue swiftly downhill to a crossroads and go right, through the gate of Pittencrieff Park. Follow the main path with views of the abbey on your right. You can visit the abbey via the Lily Pond and toilets. Otherwise, continue straight on to cross Pittencrieff Street. Go up Maitland Street and dismount to walk up the one-way Ross Lane. At the top, turn left onto Goldrum Street and after 300m follow cycle signs on the right through a small park onto William Street. Turn right and after a short distance find a car park on the left by the start of a disused railway line, now tarmac: this gives easy cycling. Leave the line after 1.5km at the sign for

Limekilns by the Firth of Forth

Crossford and turn right onto a minor road. Ahead, there are brilliant views of Edinburgh and the Pentlands on the far side of the Forth. The road plunges downhill to give the brief impression that you are flying towards the hills. Continue, more sedately, into Crossford. Turn left onto the A994, then right and downhill again to reach the busy A985. Follow the path on the right before crossing to the cycleway. After 1km, turn left and then immediately sharp left onto a muddy road. Follow the Blue Kingdom of Fife cycle signs, which lead right after 300m, to Charlestown, an eighteenth-century planned village, once important for its lime production. It is now home to the Scottish Lime Centre, and the remaining crags are loved by climbers. Be careful on the section of cobblestones: a bump gives a nasty surprise as you leave. Heading east towards the Forth Road Bridge, you soon reach the lovely village of Limekilns. In the past, Limekilns boasted an important ferry service across the Forth to Bo'ness. Robert Louis Stevenson alludes to this in Kidnapped when the central character David Balfour crosses the firth to conclude his odyssey. Accompany the shore road round the harbour, signed NCN Route 76, to pass Bruce Haven. Continue by a wall, behind which lie the eerie ivy-clad ruins of Rosyth Church. Follow the shore path until it swings inland to climb steeply up to a

busy main road. Cross the A985 with care and follow the minor road opposite, signed Pattiesmuir (ignoring the NCN Route 76 signs). Follow the Kingdom cycle and green Scotways signs onto a track ahead, signed Grange Road. After 400m veer to the right to regain a road. At a T-junction go right, past Wester Gellet, and left at the next T-junction onto a busier road. Continue for 2km onto Elgin Street. Go straight through the crossroads, encountered earlier, and climb the hill past the Andrew Carnegie Birthplace Museum to return to the station.

A round at Gleneagles

Time **3h30** Distance **40km** Terrain **Hilly;
mainly minor roads** Map **OS Landranger 58**
Access **Direct trains from Perth, Stirling,
Dundee, Glasgow Queen Street and
Edinburgh**

**This route will exercise your hamstrings
while giving a pleasing circuit through
the eastern end of the Ochils on
reasonably quiet roads.**

The flat-topped grassy Ochils, which lie to
the northeast of Stirling, were formed by a
volcanic outpouring millions of years ago.
From the south, these hills present a

formidable feature for their lowly size, with
a steep 20km escarpment line. This route
begins at Gleneagles Station (just 15
minutes by train from Perth or Stirling), by
the gentler northern edge of the hills, but
this still presents a challenge for the cyclist
The station was originally built to service
the nearby exclusive hotel.

Follow the access road to the A9 and turn
left onto a footpath. After about 500m, this
leaves the A9 at a turn-off. At the top, go
left onto the A823 and after a further 1km
or so turn left onto a smaller road, signed
Duchally Hotel. Some 3km of undulating

ground follows, before a sharp left turn takes you under a railway bridge. Continue by this road as it loops around, then at a T-junction turn right towards Dunning. The scenery changes here as the road levels beneath the northern Ochil slopes, passing a witch memorial before the village. From the centre of Dunning, head southwards on the Yetts O'Muckhart road which involves some pretty stiff climbs and long uphill sections. Take time to stop and look back over Strath Earn and beyond to the Trossachs. Soon after passing a square house on the right, you come to the crux of the climb. The road levels by Blaeberry Toll House: soon after comes your reward for all that uphill effort, with long descents through the hills and past wild glens. A steep section takes you along Glendey Burn to finish. Take a right at the next junction to meet the A823, which leads you northwestwards past

Castlehill Reservoir. Shortly after is the Tormaukin Hotel, a great place for a meal or a drink. The road beyond accompanies the river into Glen Devon with a few rises, before a long welcome descent back down to the A9 turn-off, where you retrace the route to the station.

◄ Bridge over the River Devon

69

Falkland of Fife

Time 3h Distance 33km Terrain Mostly flat
with some hilly sections; minor roads
Maps OS Landranger 58 and 59 Access
Direct trains from Perth, Dundee and
Edinburgh to Ladybank

**This circuit begins on the flat, passing
through the historically important
village of Falkland and climbing north of
Auchtermuchty before a fun descent
back to the start point of Ladybank.**

The joy of cycling from a train is clearly
illustrated by this route where, within
seconds of leaving the station at Ladybank,
you are on a quiet road. From Platform 1,
follow a ramp onto Kettle Road (or from the

other platform leave the station and turn
left to reach the same point) and then on to
Kettlebridge. Follow the road through the
village and turn right at the blue Kingdom
of Fife cycle signs for Falkland. After about
1km these lead you under a railway and on
towards Freuchie, on a stretch which can be
exposed to the wind. This first half of the
route is almost entirely level. Initially, traffic
levels are low but they do increase as you
approach Falkland. In the pretty village of
Freuchie the route merges with NCN Route
1, which you follow to Newton of Falkland.
If you fancy a short off-road section, go
right just as you leave Newton onto a minor
road and find a grassy path on the left

...fter 30m which leads to the northern edge of Falkland.

A welcome landmark for cyclists in this lovely village is the Bruce Fountain, surrounded by good pubs and eateries.

Falkland Palace, which is open to visitors, was the country residence of eight Stuart monarchs, including Mary, Queen of Scots. Once refreshed, head for Auchtermuchty on cycle paths that run north beside the B936. This quiet village boasts a trio of musical sons: the accordionist Jimmy Shand and the bespectacled Proclaimer twins. Follow cycle signs marked 'Newburgh' past the popular Cycle Tavern. Now comes the hard bit as your route starts to climb steadily uphill: ignore further NCN Route 1 cycle signs that branch left. The top of the climb is reached after 3km and from here it's a downhill stretch looking out over the Tay estuary. Slow down when you spot a village above you to the right, making a right turn here for Grange of Lindores. Now continue straight on to join a minor road, which climbs steeply before dropping down past several lochs. When you meet a T-junction, turn right onto the B-road and, after 2km, take a left turn, signposted for Collessie. The road winds round to Letham where the hills end, and you cross the A92 soon after. Next, at a staggered junction, head southwards on the minor road past wooded estates towards Pitlessie. After a railway crossing, take the next right back to Ladybank station.

St Andrews pilgrimage

Time 3h **Distance** 42km **Terrain** Hilly;
minor roads and cycle paths
Map OS Landranger 59 **Access** Direct trains
from Dundee and Edinburgh to Cupar

**A longer circular route on usually quiet
roads and cycle paths, which climbs
from Cupar before dropping down to the
golden sands of St Andrews.**

Cupar, in the heartland of Fife, is
surrounded by rich arable land. From the
train station, turn left, and take the first
turning on the left to Ceres. You're soon
above the town as the route climbs to Ceres
Moor, where the gradient eases. The road
now takes you round a sharp bend before
dropping into Ceres, a pretty village which,
unusually in Scotland, has a village green.
Ahead the quaint, Bruegelesque statuette is
said to represent the last occupant of the
Ceres Provostry. At the T-junction turn left
and continue for about 2.5km to turn left
again, this time at the crossroads in

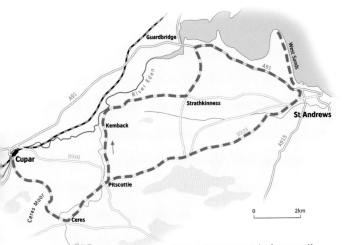

Pitscottie. Now turn immediately right onto a small road which runs along the east bank of the wooded Ceres Burn. Soon, it plunges between water-eroded limestone outcrops: a series of waterfalls accompany this pleasant section of the journey. After passing a bridge about 1km beyond Kemback (don't cross it), continue on the minor road signposted for Strathkinness which follows the River Eden for a short distance. Ahead, the road rises steeply but eases after a bend, where the sight of the sea will spur you on. There are good picnic spots just before the brow of the hill. On reaching Strathkinness, turn left by the pub on the corner to drop steadily down to the coast. Cross the main road and turn right along the pavement: this soon joins a good cycleway, part of the northbound NCN

Route 1. Continue past the famous golf links and through a gap in a wall onto a street. To visit the West Sands, go left. After you've dipped your toes in the North Sea continue to the A91, at the edge of St Andrews. Turn left, and then right onto the A915, continuing for 300m to now turn right onto the B939 and NCN Route 1 southbound. This climbs uphill past houses for 500m. At a fork go left and prepare yourself for a steady 3.5km climb. Pass Craigtoun Country Park but ignore the NCN signs pointing left. Soon the road levels and, towards the end, a succession of bike-friendly bends shuttle you back to the main road for a final downhill section to Pitscottie. Retrace the start of the route to the station from here or for a flatter but less peaceful run, turn right onto the B940 and negotiate your way through streets south of the River Eden back to Cupar station.

◀ The Crossgate in Cupar

Take off from Leuchars

Time **2h30** Distance **20km** Terrain **Flat; minor roads and cycle tracks**
Map **OS Landranger 59** Access **Direct trains from Dundee and Edinburgh to Leuchars**

An easily accessible off-road route through Tentsmuir National Nature Reserve with plenty of opportunities for wildlife spotting.

This wonderful pine forested area was previously moorland, hence the name Tents Muir. Now Tentsmuir Point National Nature Reserve boasts mature stands of Scots and Corsican pine, planted by the Forestry Commission. At the easternmost edge lies three miles of golden sand, rolling dunes and the bitingly cold North Sea. With this outlook and some superb wide forest tracks, this unspoilt area is perfect for exploration on bike. The reserve, at the mouth of the Tay Estuary, forms an important roosting and feeding area for huge gatherings of seaduck, waders and wildfowl. It is also a haul-out area for over 2000 common and grey seals. Butterflies are a feature of the grassland and dunes too. This route starts at Leuchars but can also be approached from St Andrews for a longer circuit.

◄ Leuchars Parish Church

Exit Leuchars train station on the left and cycle to meet a main road. Go left and cross over to find a grassy path by the edge of MOD housing. At the end go left onto a minor road, part of NCN Route 1. If starting from St Andrews follow NCN Route 1 to reach this point after 7km. Go past the RAF airbase and turn right at the blue Kingdom of Fife cycleway sign for Tayport onto Pitlethie Road. After 2km, go right towards Kinshaldy forest. Follow this road through dense woods to a car park, where you leave all the cars behind as the route passes by a vehicle barrier to run parallel to the hidden beach. After an enjoyable 2km stretch, you'll come to the icehouse (you can't miss it). It was used in the nineteenth century to hold caught salmon from the Tay estuary. Leave the bikes here for a stroll down to the beach. Cross a stile and follow the track beyond: the views of the sea and the vast beach as they open up take you by surprise. Chances are you'll have this to yourself too: you and the seals that is, as

nearby Tentsmuir Point attracts both grey and common seals, which come at different times between spring and autumn to moult or breed; don't disturb them. Continue around the point. After about a further 2km of cycling through pine, you'll reach a junction. Bear left (signposted Leuchars Direct Route) to follow a track, initially by the edge of fields, which will return you to the Kinshaldy beach road. From there, simply retrace your route to the station.

75

Perth and the Palace

Time 2h30 Distance 23km Terrain Hilly;
mainly quiet minor roads
Map OS Landranger 53 Access Direct
trains from Dundee, Stirling, Glasgow
Queen Street and Edinburgh to Perth

**Cross the Tay to reach Scone Palace
and the start of a testing circuit past
standing stones and through wild-
feeling country before a long swift
descent back to the station.**

Perth is an easy town to reach from all
points in central Scotland and it's equally
easy to escape from. Exit the train station
and turn left to go up Leonard Street past

the Quality Hotel and towards the building
with a green domed roof on York corner.
Turn right onto County Place and continue
east to cross the Tay on Queen's Bridge.
Now turn left onto the busy Dundee Road.
There's a cycle lane for some of the
distance to Scone Palace: follow the sign
for Scone left at a fork onto Isla Road: this
is the A93. After 1.5km, you'll pass the
gates to Scone Palace (open seasonally).
Set back from the Tay, the palace marks the
site of Scotland's ancient Pictish capital,
later overtaken by the Celts. In the ninth
century, Kenneth MacAlpin seized Scone
after becoming the first Scottish king. Many

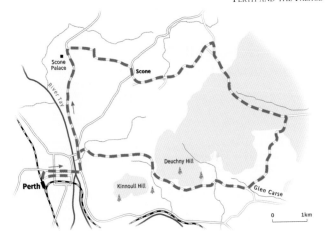

believe he brought the Lia Fáil, or Stone of Destiny, with him. In any case, from then on, Scottish kings were enthroned in front of the Palace. More recently, the gardens became recognised for their pinetum, the highlight being Scotland's oldest Douglas fir raised successfully from seed sent from America by botanist David Douglas in the early 1800s. A further 1.5km beyond the first set of palace gates, turn right for the village of Scone (signposted). A very steep section is followed by 2km of level ground which runs through Scone. When you reach a T-junction, turn right onto Angus Road and then left 300m downhill, signposted Murrayshall. Go past houses and follow the road at a bend onto the hilly Bonhard Road. Continue to a T-junction, and turn left to pass a large standing stone opposite the Murrayshall Hotel where there are good views of farmland below. Climb a bit more and keep

going to a quiet crossroads, where you should turn right. The road soon climbs again taking you into a wilder landscape with views of Pole Hill before you go right at a sign for Glen Carse. This leads onto a fun stretch which is mainly downhill and ends at a T-junction by a thatched house. A right turn brings you onto another very steep hill. Eventually, this sweeps close to Kinnoull Hill, with great views of the Tay. A long and fast downhill stretch takes you back to Perth. Turn left at a T-junction and, where this road meets the main road, go left on a cycle lane. Cross back over Queen's Bridge and turn left on a cycle lane and then right at the signs for the Ring Road (avoiding low bridge) onto Canal Street and another cycle lane. At the end of Canal Street, cross King Street and follow the narrow Hospital Street round for the last stretch to the station.

◄ Scone Palace

Fast track to Glen Almond

Time 3h30 Distance 55km Terrain Level cycle tracks and minor roads Map OS Landranger 58 and 52 Access Direct trains from Dundee, Stirling, Glasgow Queen Street and Edinburgh to Perth

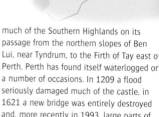

Get a clean getaway from Perth on cycle tracks before taking to quiet roads for a journey up Glen Almond.

The River Tay – Scotland's great river – is a captivating sight in any conditions, but after heavy rainfall its churning, muddied waters make an awesome spectacle. This accounts, too, for its popularity further upriver among whitewater paddlers and rafters. The Tay has by far the biggest catchment of any Scottish river, draining much of the Southern Highlands on its passage from the northern slopes of Ben Lui, near Tyndrum, to the Firth of Tay east of Perth. Perth has found itself waterlogged on a number of occasions. In 1209 a flood seriously damaged much of the castle, in 1621 a new bridge was entirely destroyed and, more recently in 1993, large parts of the town were inundated. Flood defences have since been built.

From Perth train station turn left and

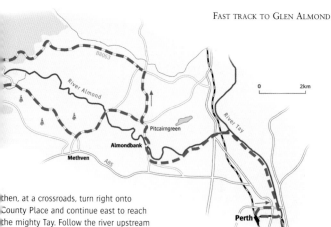

then, at a crossroads, turn right onto County Place and continue east to reach the mighty Tay. Follow the river upstream along the west bank. Rather than continuing past Perth Bridge (the more northerly of two), take a side path, opposite the Royal George Hotel, which goes under the bridge where it meets the northbound NCN Route 77. Signs lead you into North Inch Park and beyond, where this peaceful path continues alongside the river to the confluence with the River Almond. Follow Route 77 as it swings westwards along the Almond, passing under the railway and A9 bridges (this section liable to flooding) before leaving the river by minor roads and cycle tracks to cross the Almond and climb to Pitcairngreen. In the village, go up the left side of a crescent, turn left at the end and then first right. When you reach the B8063 after about 2km, turn left to leave Route 77 and head into Glen Almond, where a 9km stretch with some climbing takes you into wild country. Follow the road as it crosses back over the river and drops down into Buchanty, then turn left by a minor road, signposted for Methven. The

next undulating section is rewarded by a long downhill stretch. On reaching a T-junction, turn right and continue by minor roads to a crossroads. Turn left here to weave a winding course back over the river and into Pitcairngreen. The route now takes you past a country pub and steeply downhill. At the sharp bend, turn left onto College Mill Road where the NCN Route 77 signs begin again. Where the track leaves the river at an ambiguous marker, follow a rough path between houses, rejoining the Almond's banks further on to enjoy a stress-free return to Perth. Once you emerge from under Perth Bridge, follow the cycle lane downstream and turn right at the signs for the Ring Road (avoiding low bridge) onto Canal Street and a cycle lane. At the end of Canal Street, cross King Street and follow the narrow Hospital Street round for the last stretch to the station – where there's a great café.

◄ Glen Almond after the rain

Edinburgh is Scotland's most cycle-friendly city by a long shot and riding a bike is the perfect way to explore the city. A network of interlinking cycle paths, which follow the Union Canal, other waterways and disused railway lines allows for miles of traffic-free cycling. On road, there are comprehensive and clearly signed cycle lanes. Spokes, the Lothian Cycle Campaign, which has been instrumental in establishing Edinburgh's cycle-friendly status, publishes easy-to-follow cycle maps for the city, Midlothian, West Lothian and East Lothian.

To the south, the Pentland Hills form a softly rolling horizon and provide a haven for those who need to escape from the rigours of urban life. There are less visited places to explore, too, along the Firth of Forth and to the east by the North Sea.

One thing the seven routes in this chapter have in common is long stretches of level cycle paths. Where roads have to be followed, quiet routes are always used. The flattest sections accompany the Union Canal, a contour canal which follows the lie of the land with absolutely no hills. It passes through some surprisingly pretty countryside and offers superb crossings from a series of aqueducts, high above the tops of the trees.

The longest trip here is a cross-Scotland bike tour. Starting on the Union Canal in the heart of Edinburgh and joining the Forth & Clyde Canal by Falkirk to continue to the Clyde estuary, it offers a remarkable perspective on a rejuvenated waterway that was once the lifeblood of central Scotland.

Edinburgh and Lothian

Gearing up for Cairnpapple

Time **2h30** Distance **22km** Terrain Hilly;
minor roads Map **OS** Landranger 65 or
Spokes West Lothian Cycle Map
Access Direct trains from Edinburgh,
Glasgow Queen Street and Stirling to
Linlithgow

**The fun thing about this strenuous route
on quiet roads is that you very quickly
leave Linlithgow behind to enter the
countryside for cross-Scotland views and
hilltop Neolithic forts.**

From Linlithgow train station, head uphill
to the canal (if starting from the ticket office
side, begin by taking a left uphill through
the railway tunnel) and turn right along the
towpath. After passing under a bridge

(300m), continue for a further 400m to
cross the canal by the next road bridge and
climb past houses. The road soon steepens
severely. If you persevere, you'll find the
gradient eases at a right-hand bend by a
turning. Continue through trees. An
interesting diversion lies ahead on the left
by a wooden pagoda: this is the Korean War
Memorial. You can walk past it to find a
footpath on the slopes behind which leads,
in late summer, through flowering heather
and bilberries. A five-minute walk will take
you to the top where there are fabulous
views, given the lowly height. Away to the
east lies Bass Rock and the Pentlands, to
the north the distinctive profile of the
Southern Highlands, and out west, the

Cowal Peninsula and even Arran on a good day. Back on the bike, take the next left. Then, at a fork, take the right branch, signed Cairnpapple Hill, which is famous for its Neolithic site. It's a stiff ascent to reach the footpath immediately below the henge on the right. If you arrive outwith opening hours, it's still worth the five-minute walk from this point. The round earth-built structure is 5000 years old and regarded as one of the most important prehistoric sites on the Scottish mainland. From here, the road dips before another climb to a craggy lookout point. The road now bends round to the right, by the Knock viewpoint, for a swift descent through a lovely wooded stretch: it's fairly easy on the legs as you glide by the Bathgate Hills. Soon after you pass the Galabraes standing stone on a solitary knoll, the road descends to a T-junction. Turn left here. The hills soon give way to a long gentle descent to reach the A89. Turn left onto the busy main road (path in places) and, after 800m, take a left into Dechmont. When you reach the end of the village, turn left to follow signs for Linlithgow. This minor road is signed all of the way, climbing initially, with long inclines, past farmhouses. After a sharp bend, the road becomes more undulating and offers views of the Riccarton Hills to the left. Further on, be prepared for a big drop followed by a tight corner: this brings you to a T-junction. Turn left for a wonderful steep finish, past wild poppies in summer, and over the Union Canal by Linlithgow Canal Basin, just minutes from the station.

◄ On Cairnpapple

Going Forth to Blackness

Time **3h** Distance **17km** Terrain **Best for wide tyres** Map **OS Landranger 65 or Spokes West Lothian Cycle Map** Access **Direct trains from Edinburgh, Glasgow Queen Street and Stirling to Linlithgow**

Variety is the spice of life, which this route acknowledges with a taste of town life, the seashore and a quiet canal – all largely road-free.

Leave Linlithgow train station on the town side (ticket office rather than car park exit), and head downhill to the busy High Street. Turn left and continue until you reach the tourist information centre, then turn right to The Cross and the famous Church of St Michael of Linlithgow with its bright aluminium open crown spire, representing the crown of thorns, which can be seen from miles around. Linlithgow Palace stands next to it. Follow the path round the side of the church to descend by the Peel (parkland) and Linlithgow Loch. Curve right towards the shore by a path, which leads to Chapel Lane. At the lane's end, turn left onto the main road and then first left onto a minor road. You are instantly transported from the bustle of the town to peaceful countryside. A gentle climb follows, passing fields and farmhouses. Go left at a junction, after Bonnytoun Farm, and climb for a short distance to reach a quiet crossroads. There

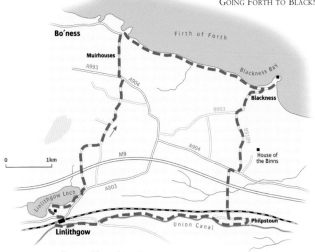

are great views all around from this point. Carry straight on to begin a fast descent. This ends by a busy main road. Turn left along this (take care here) and then cross over to follow the road past Muirhouses. Below, the Forth estuary rushes up to meet you as you whizz towards Bo'ness on a 1:10 slope. At the bottom, where the road bends sharply to the left, turn right to pass industrial units: watch out for lorries. Follow a right of way sign by a sawmill to reach the shore and hardcore paths. Continue on this quiet section. After a while, you'll come to a short flight of steps and a narrow path which runs alongside the shore. In summer, overgrown vegetation may force you to walk on the sands for a short distance. Blackness Castle soon appears. Carry straight on for a short detour to the castle or turn right through the village and left 1km further on, signposted for Edinburgh.

This long straight stretch claws back the height lost in the earlier swift descent. When you reach a T-junction, take a right and then first left to pass above the M9 and beneath the railway line: you are headed to an older transport conduit. Turn left at the next T-junction to reach the village of Philpstoun (no facilities). Turn into a housing estate by an old redbrick church. Go through an archway on the right and curve to the left past sheds. The Union Canal is reached by a ramp. Head west for a delightful unspoilt stretch by the waterway on a good earth surface. This leads to Linlithgow Basin where you can admire restored barges and sense a slower pace of life (summer boat trips and tearoom here). To return to the station, turn right down Back Station Road and then left into the car park 10m before the traffic lights.

◄ Blackness Castle on the Forth

The Union with the Forth & Clyde

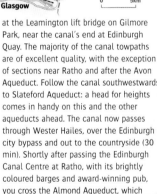

Time 7h Distance 107km
Terrain Flat; cycle paths and
some short road sections
Maps OS Landranger 66, 65 and 64
Access Direct trains from (outward)
Glasgow Queen Street, Stirling and Perth
to Edinburgh Haymarket and (return)
Bowling to Glasgow Queen Street

**Following Central Scotland's canal
network, this route offers easily the
most peaceful way to cross the country.
It is described from the east but can be
reversed to begin from Glasgow.**

Start from Edinburgh's Haymarket station.
Turn right and walk along Morrison Street.
Take the second turning on the right onto
Grove Street: you'll need to walk this too as
it's one way. At the end, go right and then
first left to join the Union Canal cycle path

at the Leamington lift bridge on Gilmore
Park, near the canal's end at Edinburgh
Quay. The majority of the canal towpaths
are of excellent quality, with the exception
of sections near Ratho and after the Avon
Aqueduct. Follow the canal southwestwards
to Slateford Aqueduct: a head for heights
comes in handy on this and the other
aqueducts ahead. The canal now passes
through Wester Hailes, over the Edinburgh
city bypass and out to the countryside (30
min). Shortly after passing the Edinburgh
Canal Centre at Ratho, with its brightly
coloured barges and award-winning pub,
you cross the Almond Aqueduct, which

curves 23m above the landscape. You'll notice there are no locks: this is a contour canal and its position is dictated by the lie of the land. Soon after passing Linlithgow and its own canal centre, cross the Avon Aqueduct (26m high), the longest in Scotland and the second tallest in the UK. Another obstacle for the engineers lies ahead: Prospect Hill, by Falkirk. A 631m tunnel passes through it (bring lights and dismount). Personally, I prefer air above my head so this route leaves the canal towpath briefly. As you near Falkirk, you will pass under a high arched bridge: leave the towpath 100m beyond this and follow an old ramp to another bridge. Go right and then left uphill on the B8028. After 1km, now going downhill, turn left onto Slamannan Road (B803) and, after 300m, look out for a green signed access point to the canal on the right. Continue to follow the canal which leads through a well-lit tunnel. On the far side, you'll see the end of the Union Canal which stops dramatically in mid-air. Originally the Forth & Clyde and Union Canals were joined by a flight of 11 locks near here, long since destroyed. A path leads easily down to the Falkirk Wheel and the Forth & Clyde Canal. Follow it left to access the towpath via a footbridge: this is open during daylight hours. For 24-hour access from the Union Canal to the Forth & Clyde Canal, you can take a signed ramp (2km from Slamannan Road access point) to Lock 16 by Camelon.

You are now halfway across Scotland. If you're fit, you can do the entire route in a day but canals are best suited to a slower pace and you could consider stopping overnight in Linlithgow and having morning coffee at the Falkirk Wheel. From here it's downhill, albeit very gradually, to the Clyde which makes for an enjoyable finish, although it is important to take the prevailing westerlies into account which may dictate a west-east crossing. The remainder of the route to Bowling on the Forth & Clyde is straightforward but full of interesting vistas. It passes under the A80, taking in Roman forts and sections of the Antonine Wall, over Dullatur bog and through Kirkintilloch. There's a watering hole and eatery at Underwood Lockhouse, west of Bonnybridge, and also on the canal by Kilsyth; the Lock Bar before Maryhill is also a good place to stop for a meal. In Glasgow, you leave the towpath briefly at Stockingfield Junction to pass under a bridge: follow Bowling signs west and enjoy increasingly good views over the city. Continue to journey's end at Bowling Basin where the canal meets the Clyde. Bowling, its train station and a faster way of life is just two minutes away. Follow signs to the road and go left to enter Bowling: the station is about 500m away on the left.

A barge at Ratho

Easy spin to Riccarton

Time 2h Distance 24km Terrain Flat;
mostly on cycle paths; short busy town
section at start and finish (can be walked)
Map Landranger 66 or Spokes Edinburgh
Cycle Map Access Direct trains from
Glasgow, Stirling and Perth to Edinburgh
Haymarket

**This route offers an easy escape route
from the city, following first the Water
of Leith and then the Union Canal for a
pleasing and easy circuit.**

Both the Union Canal and the Water of
Leith hold a central place in Edinburgh's
rich industrial heritage. The latter's many
waterwheels drove the mills that produced
paper, flour, cloth and even spices and
snuff, accounting for the growth of the
villages along its banks. The Water of Leith
Walkway, which runs alongside the river for
some 18km from Balerno to Leith, has
revived its use now as a recreational route.
Families wishing to avoid heavy traffic

should start and finish in Roseburn Park,
omitting the Union Canal section east of
Slateford to return by the Walkway.

From Edinburgh's Haymarket station, turn
left on to Haymarket Terrace and left again
just after the car park entrance to swing
around the back of the Inland Revenue
building. After passing blocks of flats, turn
left and follow this road round to Balbirnie
Place. Turn left at the main road. Pass under
an old railway bridge. At traffic lights, take
the left turning on to Roseburn Street. First
right leads to Roseburn Park: Murrayfield
Stadium lies ahead and you have left
Edinburgh's traffic behind. Follow signs for
the Water of Leith Walkway, which is on
your right. The Slateford-Gorgie section is
an important wildlife link between the
upper river and the city portion, and it may
be possible to spot heron, kingfishers and
dippers. Cross Gorgie Road to wafts of wild
garlic in the spring. Skirt around the edge of
the Chesser Allotments and continue by the

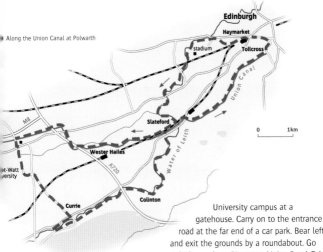

◀ Along the Union Canal at Polwarth

river to reach the grand Slateford Aqueduct (1822) and Viaduct (1847). The aqueduct holds the Union Canal which once carried barges laden with stone, grain and coal. Its nemesis, the railway, runs parallel to it. The Water of Leith Visitor Centre is on the far side. At the aqueduct, climb a series of steps to the Union Canal, and turn right. Carry on through Wester Hailes and over the Scott Russell Aqueduct, which crosses the bypass, to reach the countryside. If you have time, it's worth continuing to Ratho, home to the Bridge Inn and Edinburgh Canal Centre (boat trips from here: booking essential). Otherwise, part company with the canal at the fourth bridge (Hermiston House Road) after the aqueduct to head south. When you reach the A71 junction, turn left and cross into Heriot-Watt

University campus at a gatehouse. Carry on to the entrance road at the far end of a car park. Bear left and exit the grounds by a roundabout. Go right here, along Riccarton Mains Road. Take the next left (after about 200m), and continue on this minor road to cross a railway line. Continue straight on to find a farmhouse and Donkey Lane, which leads into a housing estate: turn left here and follow the road to exit. Cycle signs for Leith lead you across Lanark Road and to a path opposite which runs down to the river: you should accompany this downstream. The Walkway takes you through Colinton Tunnel and across the Union Canal. Leave the river here to follow the canal to Leamington Lift Bridge on Gillmore Park in the back heart of the city near the canal's end. Go left onto Gillmore Park and at its end turn right onto Dundee Street before taking the next left onto Grove Street. At the end, go left again onto Morrison Street and continue back to Haymarket.

Great Pentland escape

Time 2h30 **Distance** 22km **Terrain** Flat with one long climb; good tracks, minor roads and cycle path; best for wide-tyred bikes **Maps** OS Landranger 66 and (optional for city section only) Spokes Edinburgh Cycle Map **Access** Direct train from Edinburgh to Kingsknowe

As far as city routes go, this is one of the best with a varied mix of quiet traffic-free sections, a series of exhilarating climbs to the Pentland reservoirs and excellent views.

From Kingsknowe station, go right to cross the Union Canal and right again along the towpath. After 500m, cross a footbridge to head south on NCN Route 75, passing the ancient village of Colinton, which has been encompassed by the sprawling capital but maintains a unique identity and charm.

Its origins date to the eleventh century: the river was forded here and the parish of Hailes (Colinton's old name) grew around a long destroyed kirk. From here, the route follows the wooded Water of Leith upstream towards Balerno, passing beneath the city bypass to begin a flat, peaceful section that stretches for more than 5km. At the point where a stone wall begins, curve to the right (marked). When you come to the end of the walkway, turn left (leaving the NCN route) and take another left at the roundabout onto Balerno's pedestrianised main street. At the top, turn right onto Mansfield Road. A steady 3km of huffing and puffing will bring you past the Animal Welfare Centre with a rewarding perspective over the Forth. Further on, signs direct you through a car park on the left to Threipmuir Reservoir, behind which looms

Bringing in the bales near Balerno

ack Hill. There are a number of reservoirs
ound here, built to supply the mills with a
eady source of water after the Water of
eith proved too feeble during the summer
onths. Now, they are a haven for wildlife,
rds and fishermen alike. On the
ack, you'll have to lift your bike
ver a gate to continue by the
ide stony track to the edge
f the reservoir. Continue
the dam end, where
ou have to cross
obblestones (very
ippery after rain),
nd along the
estern side of
arlaw Reservoir to
e redbrick ranger
ation beyond. Go
rough a gate and
rn right onto a
rmac road. This takes
ou to a T-junction
00m further on, where
ou should go left and
en right. Now comes a
n downhill section with great
ews out to the Firth of Forth and
cross to Fife. After Wester Kinleith farm,
ollow the minor road straight ahead to
each Middle Kinleith. Here, the route
oubles back on itself to the right, passing
row of cottages where it becomes a track
nd continues to the pretty Clubbiedean
eservoir. Beyond this, pass Torduff
eservoir and an ornate nineteenth century

engraving. Drop steeply and cross the city
bypass by a road bridge to reach Bonaly
Road. At a staggered crossroads, continue
straight ahead onto West Mill Road. At the
bottom of a hill, slow down and take a right
turn to rejoin NCN Route 75. Turn right to
retrace your route back to the Union
Canal and the station.

91

Rolling through East Lothian

Time 3h30 Distance 33km Terrain Flat;
cycle tracks and minor roads; best suited
to wide-tyred bikes Map OS Landranger 66
or Spokes East Lothian Cycle Map Access
Direct trains from (outward) Edinburgh to
Musselburgh and (return) Longniddry
to Edinburgh

**Following cycle tracks, disused railways
and country lanes, this route offers a
quiet journey that joins the stations of
Musselburgh and Longniddry.**

The train ride from Edinburgh to seaside
Musselburgh takes just a few minutes. From
the south side of Musselburgh station, take
a track downhill parallel to the railway lines
and into a housing estate. Make two right

turns and go straight on to cross a
roundabout into Ferguson Drive. Find NCN
Route 1 at the end, following the Route 1
signs across the River Esk and then right at
a sign reading 'River Esk Path: Whitecraig'
on the far side. This leads under the A1 and
onto the rural Cowpits Road. Go right to
follow this road to a T-junction. Turn left to
pass through Whitecraig and, by the exit
speed signs, look right: Route 1 snakes
between pillars onto a pleasant narrow
track. Pass under a bridge after 1km. Some
300m further on there is a signed path for
the Pentcaitland Railway Path. This old
railway path comes alive in autumn with
blackberries, hawthorn and rosehip.
It provides pleasant cycling though the

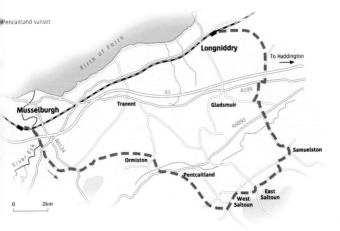

Pencaitland sunset

ack can be muddy in places. Initially, it asses through a wooded section and rther on passes the site of long bandoned coalfields. Where the path forks, o right past a memorial to Oxenford Pit. ake care just after some silos where the ath crosses a road, and beware where it rosses the busy A6093 after a hill beyond ne sewage works. Continue to the end of ne line at Saltoun station. For a spirited version, turn right and right again to lenkinchie Distillery. Otherwise go left to each West Saltoun, and continue uphill to ast Saltoun. Along the way there are good ews of the coastline. In East Saltoun, go eft by a disused fountain before turning ght after 30m to reach a lovely narrow ountry road. This makes a gradual descent

to reach a grassy triangle, where you should turn left to soon meet a larger road. Turn right on to this, taking a left at Begbie Farm after about 1.5km. After crossing a picturesque bridge, it's a steady 1km climb: continue straight ahead at the crossroads and turn left when you reach a T-junction. This road steers you round a bend before descending to the A199 and roadside cycle path. Here, take a right and then first left (signed Huntington) over the A1. Before crossing an old railway bridge, go left onto a farm road. Pass through a gate on the right to magically reach another old railway line, now a cycle path. Turn left to follow the route, where trains once clanked, to Longniddry station.

Coasting to Dunbar

Time **3h** Distance **25km** Terrain **Hilly;
coastal track and minor roads; best suited
to wide-tyred bikes** Map **OS Landranger
67 or Spokes East Lothian Cycle Map**
Access **Direct train from Edinburgh
to Dunbar**

**A varied route with steep climbs and
return coastal route to the birthplace of
John Muir, the visionary conservationist
who fought for and achieved the
preservation of many of America's wild
places in the nineteenth century.**

Dunbar claims to receive more hours of
direct sunshine per year than anywhere

else in Scotland and makes an excellent
starting point for exploring the coastline o
East Lothian and the hills further inland.

Exit the train station, turning left at the
end of Station Road, then right at a small
roundabout to reach High Street. Continue
past John Muir's birthplace and museum
further down on the left, to the end of the
road. Go right to reach Dunbar's harbours:
the main one, Victoria Harbour, is reached
by a diversion to the left while if you keep
straight ahead you'll come to the smaller
Old Harbour. Follow the coast by Lamer
Street and then turn up Woodbush Brae to
join the main road (Queen's Road). Turn le

nd then right further on at the sign for pott. It doesn't take long to get away rom it all: make sure you stop and look ack for spectacular views of the wider oastline. In the tiny village of Spott, take he first turning on the left (signed lmscleugh) to climb steeply. The route urns a sharp corner and contours around efore making a sudden descent as the oad narrows. At the bottom of this drop, he road can be submerged when the burn s in spate: a marker indicates water levels. rom the ford, there's another steep ncline. Once the road finally levels, take he next left to follow signs for Innerwick. arry straight on through the village, efore taking a left and then a right to

pass Innerwick Castle. Further on, take care in crossing the busy A1 and continue beyond to Thorntonloch and towards Torness Point with its power station which dominates the landscape.

At the end of the road, sweep left to join the John Muir Way, which the route follows around the plant: it's probably as near as any association between the conservationist and a gas-powered nuclear plant is likely to get. Follow the coastal path, which can be cycled with care. Pass the Barns Ness Lighthouse and continue to White Sands. Leave the path where you see a single-track road and barrier: this runs past the cement works. Turn right at the top to return to sunny Dunbar.

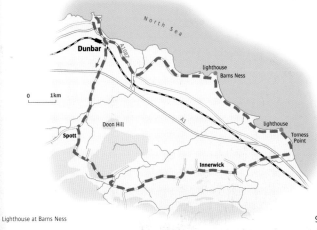

■ Lighthouse at Barns Ness

Index